So You Think You Might Like to Teach:

23 Fictional Teachers (for Real!) Model How to
Become and Remain a Successful Teacher

So You Think You Might Like to Teach:

23 Fictional Teachers (for Real!) Model How to Become and Remain a Successful Teacher

ROBERT EIDELBERG

Library of Congress Control Number:		2013903148
ISBN:	Hardcover	978-1-4797-9815-5
	Softcover	978-1-4797-9814-8
	Ebook	978-1-4797-9816-2

This book was printed in the United States of America.

Rev. date: 05/09/2013

To order additional copies of this book, contact:
Xlibris Corporation
1-888-795-4274
www.Xlibris.com
Orders@Xlibris.com
130750

DEDICATION

To my past students who challenged me – and to my current students who inspire me and keep me young. Almost everything in this book I have learned from my middle school, high school, undergraduate-level, and graduate-level students in schools I have taught in throughout that incredible classroom known as the City of New York.

In addition, this book and my soul-satisfying career as a secondary school English teacher, high school English Department chair and supervisor, and university teacher and supervisor of prospective secondary school English teachers would never have happened without the two colleagues whose teaching passion and artistry made it possible for me to become the teacher I wanted to be:

> Thank you, George Cohn, master English teacher, mentor, colleague, and founding chair of the English Department of John Bowne High School, in Flushing, New York.

> Thank you, Victor Teich, master English teacher, documentary filmmaker, colleague, and friend who every day at John Bowne High School made it look so easy because it was so well planned.

Finally, very special thanks for their teaching insights into the creation of this book to: Frank Fusco, Arlene Kase, Dr. Mal Largmann, Karen Rabinowitz, Phoebe Tuite, and my recent seminar students in the School of Education at Hunter College of The City University of New York.

Contents

ABOUT THE AUTHOR

A former journalist, Robert Eidelberg served for nineteen and a half years as the assistant principal, supervision, and chair of the English department, the performing arts department, and the library media center of William Cullen Bryant High School in New York City and a total of 32 years as a secondary school English teacher in the New York City public school system.

Upon "graduating" from Bryant High School, Mr. Eidelberg was an educational and editorial consultant and author for Amsco School Publications and a writing instructor at Audrey Cohen Metropolitan College of New York as well as at Queensborough Community College of The City University of New York.

For the past 15 years, Mr. Eidelberg has been a college adjunct both supervising and teaching undergraduate and graduate student teachers in secondary English education for The State University of New York at New Paltz and for The City University of New York at its Queens College and Hunter College campuses.

As a working author, Mr. Eidelberg is currently rethinking and revising his self-help book on critical thinking, **Playing Detective: A Self-Improvement Approach to Becoming a More Mindful Thinker, Reader, and Writer By Solving Mysteries**. He lives in the Park Slope neighborhood of Brooklyn, New York, with his life partner of 40 years and their part-hound, part-Doberman dog Marlowe, worthy successor to Cinder and Apollo.

INTRODUCTION TO A
CAREER AND A CALLING

I began teaching in 1964 and am still at it. Thanks to the values of my parents and my maternal grandmother (Beba), as well as to their high expectations for me, I learned at a young age that no matter how old I got, I would always be a student. Later I learned that I would always be a teacher.

Not only is that combination of student and teacher an unbeatable one, it is a necessary one if by a "successful" teacher we mean a person whose humanity is expressed through what is both a calling and a career. (Geoffrey Chaucer put it more poetically in The Canterbury Tales: "And gladly would he learn, and gladly teach.")

So You Think You Might Like to Teach: 23 Fictional Teachers (for Real!) Model How to Become and Remain a Successful Teacher is a book about answering the call to become a teacher and then learning to be a truly effective one (whatever your subject area specialty).

To help you achieve these personal and professional career goals, So You Think You Might Like to Teach features the middle school and high school classroom experiences of 23 fictional teachers and examines, through extended commentaries, the theoretical and practical lessons these men and women learned from their successes and failures. These role models from contemporary and classic works of literature may not be *actual* but they are quite *real*, and although some of these teachers may be larger than life, all of them are true to life, flaws and all.

I've chosen these particular 23 "novel" teachers for you to learn from because *you think* you might like to teach and *I believe* that they have a lot to offer the possible teacher, the starting-out teacher, and the novice teacher already fearing early burnout. I also trust that you would like to become the best possible teacher you can be: your joy in your career and your students' joy in their learning will depend on it.

And so, as a teacher of students and a teacher of teachers, I wish you the best should you decide to profoundly affect the lives of, let's say, 151 very special human beings in some future school year: 150 secondary school students – and you, their teacher.

Robert Eidelberg

"I paused and looked around the classroom again. Some of the students were writing down what I was telling them; others were looking at me. There were both interested and glassy gazes turned on me – more interested ones than glassy ones, I tried to tell myself, realizing at the same time that it no longer made much difference to me"

– a severely burned out teacher in the 2012 novel THE DINNER, by Herman Koch (translated from the Dutch by Sam Garrett)

1

Teacher, "know thyself"

Teachers from half a dozen different novels can get you really thinking about the character and personality traits that make a person more or less likely to succeed as a teacher and not burn out

Cast of Characters

Rick Dadier, from <u>The Blackboard Jungle</u> by Evan Hunter, United States, 1954 (*fictional teacher #1*)

"A teacher," from <u>The Friend of Women</u> by Louis Auchincloss, United States, 2007 (*fictional teacher #2*)

Theophilus North, from <u>Theophilus North</u> by Thornton Wilder, United States, 1973 (*fictional Teacher #3*)

Mr. Chips, from <u>Good-bye, Mr. Chips</u> by James Hilton, Great Britain, 1934 (*fictional teacher #4*)

Ella Bishop, from <u>Miss Bishop</u> by Bess Streeter Aldrich, United States, 1933 (*fictional teacher #5*)

E. R. Braithwaite, from <u>To Sir, With Love</u> by E. R. Braithwaite, Great Britain, 1959 (*semi-fictional teacher #6*)

Introduction to "teacher, know thyself"

So you think you *might* like to teach? If you've gone public with your thoughts, you might hear from some friends and family members that they actually consider you "a born teacher"; others, whatever their reasons, might bluntly tell you, "Think again!"

The good news for those of you not sure whether you are suited to teaching – let alone *called* to it – is that there are very few "born teachers." The bad news – as you might have guessed – is that there are very few "born teachers."

All across the country today there are classrooms of people who have gone as far as to enroll as students in bachelor's and master's degree programs in Schools of Education. They're in school to *learn* whether they want to spend at least the first few years of their professional lives – in school. Students once again – but this time *of* teaching.

In a "novel" approach, this book will introduce you to a large number of fictional teachers (for real!) in order to help you decide to teach or not to teach – as well as to help you avoid imminent burnout if you're already into the first years of what you had hoped would be a long and successful career in teaching.

Although these "novel" teachers are not *actual*, they are very, very *real*. And there is no need for you to have ever met them in their respective novels. In truth, you will immediately recognize them, as well as the school situations they find themselves in and the problems they and their students face. As potential or fairly new teachers, all you have to do as a reader of this book is to make believe – with your mind, your heart, and your soul – that you *are them*; if you do that, you will ultimately be able to decide whether you want to *be like them*. This "sort of self-help book" asks you to walk awhile in these fictional teachers' shoes so that you can assess how comfortable or uncomfortable you feel. Do you and teaching make a good fit?

So you think you might like to teach – and might possibly be good at it. It's even conceivable – but not at all necessary for the purposes of this book – that you are one of those "undecideds" sitting right now in a college classroom with other education majors just months away from your degree and your credentials. You look around the room and you know you are in good company: seemingly dedicated students with the apparent potential to become devoted teachers; eager educators just waiting for the chance to – what are the words most often heard in novels and films that feature teachers? – "mold young minds." No question that, on good days, you believe you *know* you can teach. And look around: you are not in a class by yourself.

Introduction to Rick Dadier of <u>The Blackboard Jungle</u> (in novelistic print and on the movie screen)

Rick Dadier is a first-year teacher with an "ed" school degree and student teaching experience in Evan Hunter's novel *The Blackboard Jungle*. Rick values his chosen profession as a high school English teacher as "worthwhile" and "worthy" and has thrown himself, as he puts it, into molding "the clay of undeveloped minds," confident of his chances of success.

Being self-evaluative by nature (a good quality in a teacher), Rick engages in periodic "musings." His thoughts take him back a year to some of his fellow "ed" course students and forward to some of his current, more veteran, colleagues. Rick wonders why different individuals decide to become teachers. Wouldn't you? Don't you?

Rick considers some of his former "ed" classmates and current colleagues to be "meatheads," yet he wonders whether it's right for him to condemn those who "drift into the teaching profession, drift into it because it offers a certain amount of paycheck-every-month security, vacation-every-summer luxury, or a certain amount of power, or a certain easy road when the other more difficult roads are so full of ruts?"

Not surprisingly, Rick doesn't consider himself a "meathead." He believes that he "had honestly wanted to teach." He also had no illusions about his own capabilities. He muses that he "could not paint, or write, or compose, or sculpt, or philosophize deeply, or design tall buildings. He could contribute nothing to the world creatively, and this had been a disappointment to him until he'd realized he could be a big creator by teaching. For here," he concludes, "were minds to be sculpted, here were ideas to be painted, here were lives to shape."

To spend his life as something like "a bank teller or an insurance salesman" had seemed an utter waste to Rick so he "seized upon teaching, seized upon it fervently, feeling that if he could take the clay of undeveloped minds, if he could feel this clay in his hands, could shape this clay into thinking, reacting, responsible citizens, he would be creating."

A commentary on "teacher, know thyself"

Although he does not yet have children of his own (his wife is pregnant), the teacher in Rick Dadier sees the necessary connection between other people's children that his colleagues teach and *his* future children that they and others like them might teach: teach unto other parents' children as you would want your children's teachers to teach unto yours.

Consequently, the thought of certain of his "ed" school classmates' becoming teachers is upsetting to Rick, but we need to get beyond Rick's feelings about the "meatheads" in education in order to examine the implied question behind his musings: what kind of person is right for "the calling" of teaching. *You* should know *whether* you are suited for teaching. *You* should know *why* you are suited for teaching. *You* should know *how* you are suited for teaching.

"Know thyself."

How "fervent" are you about teaching? How passionate are you about your subject area? How much do you enjoy being around young people, around teenagers? Do you think a lot about getting "burned out"?

"Know thyself."

How seriously do you want to be a teacher? How idealistic or realistic would you say you are about your reasons for thinking you might like to become a teacher? On a scale of from 1 to 5 (with five being the most strongly felt positive feeling), you should be concerned about any scores below four.

"Know thyself."

Do you see teaching, as Rick does, as a way for you to have the ability and opportunity to take and feel "the clay of undeveloped minds" in your hands and "shape this clay into thinking, reacting, responsible citizens"? If you do, do you worry about being up to the challenge of those individual "clays" that you may not be able to mold? (In Louis Auchincloss's novella *The Friend of Women*, a male "Teacher" in a New York City "private day school for young ladies" recognizes that "there were clays capable of resisting the deftest of hands.")

To continue the process of getting to know yourself as a potential teacher, you might want to ask yourself, as Rick does, whether you could see yourself spending your "allotted time on earth as a bank teller or an insurance salesman." Like Rick, would you consider these jobs "an utter waste" of your life? Can you say why? And like Rick, does it bother you that some of your fellow teachers became teachers for what you would consider "the wrong reasons"? Why is that?

Finally, within this process of "know thyself," let's do what at first glance might seem to be a strange thing at this juncture in your life: *let's consider what you would have become if you hadn't decided to become a teacher.* Actually, we began this process with your thinking about a possible life as a bank teller or insurance salesman.

Introduction to the nine ambitions of Theophilus North (whose teaching career "goes south")

Now, to throw ourselves more fully into the process, we need to meet Theophilus North, the title character in the novel *Theophilus North* by Thornton Wilder. As early as the age of 12, the young North resolves to become "a saint," seeing himself as a missionary among what he benightedly terms "primitive peoples." Eventually, over the course of the rest of his adolescence, North aspires to a grand total of nine (9!) different careers (or "ambitions" as he calls them) – among them actor, detective, and magician.

By his early 20's North is still "indeterminate" about a professional life and backs into teaching as "a safety-net." Though those words and the act they describe might sound cynical to you, it is not hard to imagine North totaling up his personal qualities and abilities and advising himself, "Well, you could always become a teacher." Spoken with a strangely mixed tone of hope and despair, these words can still constitute "we-mean-well" advice in American society and American novels. In fact, the idea that as a fallback position a person with some college education "could always become a teacher" may have been instrumental in the decision of some of Rick Dadier's colleagues in *The Blackboard Jungle* to do just that.

To help you to "know thyself" as a teacher, you might want to reflect on which of North's nine "ambitions" that he had been "afire with" are most like teaching, and which least like it. Some similarities should strike you almost at first glance, while others may take some creative imagining.

As mentioned, North's earliest ambition, he reveals "with shame," was to become "a saint." He notes that although he had never met a saint, having only read and heard about them "a great deal" while attending a school in North China where the parents of all of his fellow-students and, in a way, his teachers, were missionaries. He adds that he saw himself as "a missionary among primitive peoples," realizing, with shock, that the missionaries to the Chinese people, "perhaps covertly," regarded the Chinese as a primitive people.

Knowing better, North still "clung to the notion that I would be a missionary to a really primitive tribe. I would lead an exemplary life and perhaps rise to the crown of martyrdom." However, gradually over the next decade, North becomes aware of "the obstacles" in his path and realizes that he is "incapable of meeting the strictest demands of selflessness, truthfulness, and celibacy."

"Perhaps," he adds, "as a consequence of this brief aspiration I retained through life an intermittent childishness. I had no aggression and no competitive drive. I could amuse myself with simple things, like a child playing on the seashore with shells."

North sees his second ambition to be an anthropologist among primitive peoples as a secularization of his first ambition to be a missionary, adding that all his life he has "returned" to that interest: "The past and the future are always *present* within us."

North's third ambition was to be an archeologist, and his fourth, during his third year in college, to be "an amazing detective." He tells us that he read widely in both fictional and scientifically factual detective works. He saw himself as "Chief Inspector" North, who would "play a leading role among those who shield our lives from the intrusions of evils and madness lurking about the orderly workshop and home."

North's fifth ambition was to be "an amazing actor"; his sixth, a magician. As to the latter, he tells us that he early discovered that he had "a certain gift for soothing, for something approaching mesmerism," as though he was "driving out demons."

North's seventh ambition was to be a kind of "lover," but not an "omnivorous lover like Casanova."

North's eighth ambition was to be a rascal, which he defined as someone who lives by his wits, "one step ahead of the sheriff," without plan, without ambition, at the margin of decorous living, delighted to outwit the clods, the prudent, the money-obsessed, the censorious, the complacent."

North concludes by saying that his eighth ambition leads him into his "last and overriding one," that of a free man; he also asks us to notice all the ambitions he did not entertain: "I did not want to be a banker, a merchant, a lawyer, nor to join any of those life-careers that are closely bound up with directorates and boards of governors – politicians, publishers, world reformers. I wanted no boss over me, or only the lightest of supervisions. All these aims, moreover, had to do with people – but with people as individuals."

A commentary on knowing who you are NOT

Perhaps as you reflected on future teacher Theophilus North's original nine ambitions, you recalled certain career possibilities from your own adolescence and young adulthood. Besides teaching, that is. No doubt you noticed – perhaps for the first time – some ways in which these other career possibilities of yours are similar to teaching. (Striking differences among them were probably more evident to you long ago.)

Let's suppose you had *not* decided to become a teacher – or that teaching was not at the top of your priority list of professions and that you only became a teacher because your original choice was unrealizable for some reason. What was that other profession? If others knew you as well as you know yourself (or better!), could they have "guessed" this other profession of yours? Can you explain why?

This indirect approach to knowing yourself as a teacher may seem perverse to you – why not just ask you to think right off about why you decided to become a teacher? Yet, having you start with your other possible career choices can give insight into: some of your key character and personality traits; the kinds of situations you like or dislike to be in; and the way you care to relate to other people and other types of people. In short, the contours of your mind, heart, and soul. North has this insight when he realizes that working as an anthropologist among "primitive" peoples – an interest he says he has "returned to" all his life – is a secularization of his first impulse to become a missionary (followed by sainthood).

Perhaps, too, as you considered his "nine ambitions," you were struck by the fact that in becoming a teacher, North, in a very real sense, did become a kind of saint, a type of anthropologist, a form of detective, a manner of magician. So, how is becoming a teacher not so different from realizing certain of North's other ambitions?

If you have a second look at them, you may discover that people working in these fields are "people" people – people who seem to share an interest in others as individuals; they also seem to have a fascination with how individual people "work" – a determination to get to the bottom of what makes a person "tick." Sound at all like a teacher? And is it too "amazing" to argue that being a teacher is also like being a "rascal" ("the man who lives by his wits . . . delighted to outwit the clods") or like being a "lover" (one who is "loving")?

Finally, if you want to really run with this idea, you could try to explain to North how all nine of his ambitions can be found wrapped up in the noble profession of teaching. Care to give it a go? If you do, you may also be going a long way toward explaining to yourself what it is about *you* and about teaching that makes that coupling a good match.

Although, as comic writer and filmmaker Woody Allen famously put it, "90 percent of life is showing up," we should, as aspiring teachers, know as much as we possibly can about both our own individual human nature and about the nature of the particular line of work we're getting into. Of course, we can't know all the answers, but we should be grappling with all the key questions.

Some teachers make it a practice of *asking their students* on the first day of class to share with them orally or in writing what they think the qualities of a good teacher are in their particular subject area. But for now, why do *you* want to go into teaching? What do you want to *put into* it? What do you want to *get out of* it – for yourself and for others? How similar – or different – were your reasons for considering certain other career choices? How well suited were you for these other professions, and why is that? What are your particular personality strengths, and are they a good match for teaching?

How do you feel (and react) when people quote to you the infamous canard "Those who can, do; those who can't, teach"? Do you mount the barricades, arguing that teaching *is* an act of "doing" – in fact, a quite difficult "doing" that few of them would probably succeed at? Do you tell them about the accomplishments of one or two of these "doers" – superb teachers you had as a student in middle school or high school or college? Isn't it possible that your decision to become a teacher was influenced by these role models? Did a "remarkable" teacher make you think, "This is the life for me"?

Hello, Mr. Chips (have you ever met him in print or on the screen?)

Perhaps you experienced a Mr. Chipping? Mr. Chipping? Or do you know him as that British teacher, Mr. Chips – probably the most famous teacher in literature and film in the English language? Immortalized by James Hilton in his novel *Good-bye, Mr. Chips*, Chips is a composite of Hilton's father, and a Latin teacher at the boarding school Hilton attended, and, more generally and importantly, all devoted teachers around the world. That this nineteenth-century teacher of Latin has an affectionate nickname (even his new wife calls him Mr. Chips because his students always have) almost says it all. But not quite.

In the following view of Mr. Chips at the time of his second and final retirement from Brookfield (a boarding school for boys), certain personal and professional qualities should be evident that would cause the school to ask this remarkable teacher to come out of his first retirement: "Obedience he had secured, and honor had been granted him; but only now came love, the sudden love of boys for a man who was kind without being soft, who understood them well enough, but not too much, and whose private happiness linked them with their own." Did you have a "Mr. Chips" in your life that might have caused you to want to emulate him or her?

A commentary on the universal and timeless Mr. Chips and on his female counterpart, the remarkable Miss Ella Bishop (teaching in the high school she's just graduated from)

When American readers of *Good-bye, Mr. Chips* wrote to tell its British author that they were convinced that it was *they in the United States* who had been taught by the original Mr. Chips, Hilton commented: "I believe those letters from readers have told the truth, and that my tribute to a great profession has fitted a great many members of it everywhere."

In addition to certain qualities you believe you share with good teachers everywhere (including those in novels), do certain negative qualities in the less-than-satisfactory teachers you've experienced help you to be more aware of some of your own qualities that need to be addressed? After a mere four and a half years, Theophilus North in the Thornton Wilder novel found himself disenchanted with teaching; he had turned "cynical" and become "almost totally bereft of sympathy for any other human being" except members of his own family. In sharp contrast, many veteran teachers will tell you that teaching adolescents is the very thing that has kept them feeling and looking young.

In short, it is provocative in the best sense of the word for you to do as much thinking as you can about the human qualities – positive and less so – that you bring to teaching. Lives are at stake – yours, and your future students.

In Bess Streeter Aldrich's novel *Miss Bishop*, the president of Midwestern College tells Ella Bishop why he is offering her a job teaching English grammar at the same secondary school she has just completed being a student in: "I have watched you for four years, Miss Ella. You have done good work in grammar. You have a keen mind, an open heart, an enviable disposition, and that something which seems to me the very soul of the teaching profession – a keen interest in your fellow man." Why would you have felt honored by these reasons?

If the commendable qualities of America's Ella Bishop remind you of Britain's Mr. Chips, you will not be surprised to learn that Miss Bishop, over the years, came to be regarded as "the female and American Mr. Chips." And, as the president of Midwestern College suggests in his the-job-is-yours tribute to Miss Bishop, that last quality – "a keen interest in your fellow man" – would seem to make the preceding four qualities possible. It is the soil in which the others take root and flourish.

Meet E. R. Braithwaite (actual British teacher, as well as semi-fictionalized one in print and on the screen)

Also not surprisingly, it is largely these same qualities that the students of the East London high school in the highly autobiographical novel *To Sir, With Love* come to recognize and honor in *their* teacher, Mr. Braithwaite. Their tribute occurs at the end of the novel when the graduates present Braithwaite with a "parcel" that has a large label pasted on it "inscribed 'TO SIR, WITH LOVE' and underneath, the signatures of all of them."

Braithwaite has come to think of his students as his "children." And when Miss Bishop retires from teaching after a long and happy "life in school," she feels "like a mother" as "she watched the last child break the tie which bound it to home."

But what about Theophilus North, our "ambitious" fictional teacher?

North goes from a full-time teaching position in an all-boys prep school in New Jersey to part-time work as a one-on-one professional tutor in the mid-west. North elects tutoring over teaching in order to be a free man ("not caged and incarcerated"). For similar reasons, North never had a desire to become any of the following professions: "a banker, a merchant, a lawyer, a politician, a publisher, a world reformer." And he specifies why: he could take "no boss over me, or only the lightest of supervisions."

You might want to ask yourself what it means to you to be "free" in your professional life. Is this something you want? Is this something that teaching can give you?

Know thyself: free to be who and free to do what – in that classroom of yours as you close the door, neatly print your name on the board, and greet your students for the first time – and every time thereafter?

Consider what Miss Bishop thinks she was free to be and do as a teacher

At a surprise retirement party given for her, Miss Bishop waxes philosophical (to herself): "Before she passed from their lives she must teach them one thing more . . . these men and women she loved. But how could she approach it? What could she say? She looked over the vast sea of faces. No, it was too late. You cannot teach a great truth like that in the space of a few moments. You may only accomplish it, little by little, day by day, over a long period of time. If she had not done so by example and precept in a half-century's teaching, she could not do so now. And perhaps she had. God knew."

A commentary on teaching "by example and precept"

As you further explore your possible future as a teacher, you can't do much better than to let Miss Bishop's wisdom inform and instruct your reading, your thinking, your learning, and your early teaching. What you will accomplish you will accomplish "little by little, day by day, over a period of time," and you will do it "by example and precept."

And what would you say the "great truth" was for Miss Bishop? And what would you say the "great truth" might be for you? It may be difficult for you to get your mind around these ideas right now as you start your journey. In all likelihood, you are "anxious" in both meanings of this unusual word: "eager" to begin and "nervous" about it.

As an alternative, you might want, instead, to get in touch with your feelings as we rejoin the first fictional teacher we met in this book. Just before coming home armed with champagne and roses to celebrate with his pregnant wife that he "got the job!" Rick Dadier from *The Blackboard Jungle* stops by the empty room that will soon contain his very first class of students:

> The room was absolutely silent. The sun streamed through the windows, and the dust motes floated lazily on the broad golden beams. There was something almost sanctified about the room at this moment, and Rick walked solemnly to his desk and looked out over the rows of empty seats, feeling something like a priest in a new parish awaiting his Sunday congregation.

2

Who do you think *you*
are in the classroom?

*Seven teachers from five novels are spotlighted in their pedagogical persona – their
teacher identity – so that you can begin to grapple with what will be an ongoing question in
your professional life: "Who do you think* you *are in the classroom?"*

Cast of Characters

Malachy Dudgeon and Headmaster Bell, *from* <u>The Dead School</u> *by Patrick McCabe, Ireland,
1995 (fictional teachers #7 and #8)*

**Miss Jean Brodie and her supervisor, the headmistress of the Marcia Blaine School for
Girls**, *from* <u>The Prime of Miss Jean Brodie</u> *by Muriel Spark, Great Britain, 1961
(fictional teachers #9 and #10)*

Sy Levin, *from* <u>A New Life</u> *by Bernard Malamud, United States, 1961 (fictional teacher #11)*

Lou Savoldi, Bob Canning (and Rick Dadier), *from* <u>The Blackboard Jungle</u> *by Evan Hunter,
United States, 1954 (fictional teachers #12 and #13)*

Mr. Chips, *from* <u>Good-bye, Mr. Chips</u> *by James Hilton, Great Britain, 1934*

Introduction to *"who do you think* you *are in the classroom?"*

As you turned the page from the last – and we hope "inspiring" – words
of Chapter 1 to the opening of Chapter 2, something truly magical (and
unfortunately fictional, in this case) happened to you: you arrived at the moment
when you will meet the first students of what you hope will be a long and fulfilling
career in teaching. (You will never forget these students no matter how many years
you teach and, in some individual cases, no matter how hard you try.)

Some of these first students may be just a few years younger than you and may
very well look older. In fact, there was a time when particularly young-looking male

teachers starting out in high school were often advised to age their appearance by growing whatever facial hair they could muster. First-time teachers used all kinds of strategies to not look like their students' older brother or sister.

Also around this time, as far as the heads of the majority of secondary schools were concerned, the absolute key to your pedagogical persona – your teacher identity – was to come across as much as possible as a mature grown-up, an authoritative adult, these young people's "parent." Perhaps you have heard the Latin phrase "in loco parentis." The "loco" in this phrase does not mean that someone might be "crazy"; instead, it refers to "location" – as in "place."

Both in essence and in effect, much of society and many of its laws continue to this day to view teachers as authoritative parental figures for the children in their care – "in the parents' place" – whenever the "kids" are out of the home and in temporary residence in the school building or under teacher supervision during a school-sponsored trip. (First rule of trips: don't lose anyone!)

A commentary on "in loco parentis" as we meet novice and non-authoritative teacher Malachy Dudgeon and Headmaster Bell

In Patrick McCabe's novel *The Dead School*, which is set in a parochial "middle" school in Ireland, the school's headmaster or principal (Mr. Bell) and one of its newest teachers, Malachy Dudgeon, do not see eye to eye on what Mr. Dudgeon's pedagogical persona in the classroom should be. Headmaster Bell tells Mr. Dudgeon: "We are in loco parentis here, Mr. Dudgeon. We have duties. A relaxed attitude may be perfectly fine in college. But not here. Children need consistency. Firmness. They need someone they can look up to. Do you understand me?"

Having informally observed Malachy Dudgeon's pedagogical persona in the classroom since hiring him earlier in the semester, Headmaster Bell, as Mr. Dudgeon's boss and supervisor, does not at all professionally approve of what he has seen. In fact, if Headmaster Bell were to challengingly (and perhaps snidely) ask Mr. Dudgeon the question that makes up the essence of the title of this chapter – "who do you think you *are*?" – it is likely that he would hear back from Mr. Dudgeon what both Mr. Bell and Mr. Dudgeon know is the wrong answer for this Irish parochial school. (Can you hear in your mind's ears Mr. Bell come down hard on Mr. Dudgeon with a "where-do-you-come-off!" or a "where-do-you-get-your-nerve!" criticism of Mr. Dudgeon's teacher identity?)

In your first year as a teacher, you would not want to find yourself in this kind of relationship with your immediate supervisor. It could turn out to be your last year as well. Frustrated, Mr. Bell cannot stress enough the importance of the proper fit between teacher and school: "But not here," Headmaster Bell explains at one point, faulting Malachy Dudgeon for his failure to come across to his charges as sufficiently authoritative and "parental." And Headmaster Bell does not beat around the bush: he specifically criticizes Mr. Dudgeon's "relaxed attitude" as not appropriate in a school whose authoritative administration believes that children "need someone they can look up to" as a role model. (If you were a student in *The Dead School*, do you think *you* might slip and call Mr. Dudgeon by his given name ("Malachy") in class? If so, you've just made Headmaster Bell's case stronger.)

As a possible future teacher, how much truth do you see in Headmaster Bell's specific criticisms? How might you defend Mr. Dudgeon and perhaps save him his job – if you believe it should continue to be his? (*You* can't have it; it's all the way over in Ireland!)

You might also wonder whether Malachy Dudgeon's *students* see in him the same failings that Headmaster Bell sees.

It turns out that they do; they do not take to Mr. Dudgeon's pedagogical persona (and one way they show it is by sometimes referring to him as "Dudgy"). Here's the problem with "Dudgy"'s teacher persona from the perspective of his students:

> It was only teachers like Dudgy you didn't like because they weren't really like teachers . . . because it was so easy to annoy them. If you wanted to annoy them all you had to do was keep putting up your hand and ask questions over and over again, especially if you didn't want to know the answers. Kyle and Stephen and Pat liked doing that. They liked it when they made Mr. Dudgeon lose his voice. They sort of smiled when he lost it. It was funny when they did that because it made him lose it even more.

A commentary on teachers "who weren't really like teachers"

It's unanimous. The headmaster and Malachy's students agree: "Dudgy" and "his" school are a bad match. Not only doesn't Malachy fit his school's prescribed image of the teacher as authority figure, he doesn't believe in it philosophically. Worse, Malachy's relaxed attitude, more typical of college professors, doesn't work for this school's young students because they are not accustomed to – and consequently are thrown by and don't want – teachers who "weren't really like teachers." As Headmaster Bell actually wondered, who does Malachy think he is in the classroom – a college professor?

There's a lesson to be learned in this: as a prospective teacher, you not only need to "know thyself" and your teacher persona; you also need to know "your" school and how well you and it fit. A teacher's persona does not operate in a vacuum. (Much more about this in Chapter 5.)

Meet Miss Jean Brodie (in her prime) and her supervisor, the Headmistress of the Marcia Blaine School for Girls

The teacher named in the title of Muriel Spark's novel *The Prime of Miss Jean Brodie* provides a striking contrast to Malachy Dudgeon – or does she? At the Marcia (suitably pronounced MAR-see-a) Blaine School for Girls in Edinburgh, Scotland, students certainly "look up to" Miss Jean Brodie as an authority figure.

While the novel tells us quite directly a number of particulars about the Brodie girls, it is also very revealing *indirectly* about the woman around whom a cult of personality has formed:

> These girls formed the Brodie set. That was what they had been called even before the headmistress had given them the name, in scorn, when they moved from the Junior to the Senior school at the age of twelve. At that time they had been immediately recognisable as Miss Brodie's pupils, being vastly informed on a lot of subjects irrelevant to the authorised curriculum, as the headmistress said, and useless to the school as a school.

A commentary on "the cult of personality" in the classroom

Here's what the novel has to say about the Brodie set four years later:

> By the time they were sixteen, and had reached the fourth form . . . and had adapted themselves to the orthodox regime, they remained unmistakably Brodie, and were all famous in the school, which is to say they were held in suspicion and not much liking. They had no team spirit and very little in common with each other outside their continuing friendship with Jean Brodie. She still taught in the Junior department. She was held in great suspicion.

The six girls hand-picked by Jean Brodie as her "set" regard Jean Brodie with the kind of excessive and extreme admiration that borders on a cult. And it's no wonder, since as a teacher Jean Brodie plays at being God.

The time is the 1930's, and Jean Brodie is at the point in her life that both she and "her girls" recognize as her "prime." As Miss Brodie instructs all her day school charges, whether or not they are in her "set": "It is important to recognise the years of one's prime, always remember that."

Within a few years, though, one member of Miss Brodie's exclusive set "betrays" her, resulting in Jean Brodie's dismissal from the school. (Miss

Brodie's own word for this is not "betrays" but "assassinates" – and the term is telling.) Which of these six very different girls does the deed – and why – helps to explain the hold that Miss Brodie has had on all six of them ever since they came under her powerful influence. (No spoiler alert: it is definitely worth reading the novel *The Prime of Miss Jean Brodie* to find out the why behind which girl it turns out to be.)

To begin to understand Jean Brodie's self-image, her conception of her vocation as a teacher, and her mission to be a model to her students, it helps to single out one of her signature lines: "I am putting old heads on your young shoulders, and all my pupils are the crème de la crème."

Certainly an impressionable adolescent would feel special ("teacher's pet"?) knowing that the most fascinating teacher in the school has seen in her what she herself wasn't confident she had. Yet, surely, a responsible teacher would question whether her role is to make her students into a younger improved version of herself. (Let's note, in passing, that *some parents* do attempt this.)

Clearly the more conventional leadership of the Marcia Blaine School for Girls would frown on a Jean Brodie. Yet, the highly unorthodox Miss Brodie regularly manages both to foil the school administration's "plots to remove her" and to get away with ignoring the headmistress's "suggestions" that she leave voluntarily by applying for "a post at one of the more progressive schools," where her methods are likely to be more suitable. Although Miss Brodie finds these "suggestions" beneath her consideration, they are not above her contempt: "I shall not apply for a post at a crank school. I shall remain at this education factory. There needs must be a leaven in the lump." ("Leaven" is a substance that lightens the weight of something oppressively heavy and rises through it and above it.)

In today's educational system, first-year teachers are likely to hear – sometimes repeatedly during the first week of teacher orientation – all about a school's "mission" and its "mission statement." Miss Brodie has her own mission – and mission statement – as she declares in another of her several signature lines: "Give me a girl at an impressionable age, and she will be mine for life."

This is more than mere role modeling. Secure in her pedagogical persona, Jean Brodie is, from her point of view, the one saving grace in the stultifyingly conventional "factory" of education known as the Marcia Blaine School for Girls. Miss Brodie is convinced that she belongs at Marcia Blaine, that she is needed there (meant to be there) as this "lump"-of-a-school's "leaven." To her mind, Jean Brodie neither fits in nor belongs in some trendy, so-called progressive school, which she dismisses as all show and no substance.

In fact, Miss Brodie sees herself as the actual "progressive"; her purpose in life is to embody what she believes as a person and as a teacher to be truly "substantial," in contrast to what she believes to be the surface education that passes for substance at the Marcia Blaine School for Girls.

As a captivating cult figure for her students, Jean Brodie considers herself a rebel with a cause – and she is "disturbing." Literally. The whole point of her professional (and personal) life seems to be to make an indelible "disturbance" in the traditional way that schools educate the next generation.

For most people, the word "disturbance" generally carries a negative connotation, as suggested in one dictionary's definition of the word as "the disruption of a peaceful or ordered environment." However, some of the best, most creative teachers in today's schools would argue that the true purpose of education is *to disturb*: to shake up literal student "thoughtlessness" with questions, problems, purposeful perplexities, and calculated confusions; to get students to acknowledge uncertainty as the foundation for learning (ignorance is not bliss; to be alive is not to go around "ignoring" your world); to use a wedge on a locked door when you can't come up with the key; to take nothing for granted.

To "disturb" the ordered world of a student's conventional thinking is exactly what good teaching is about – and in pursuit of that goal, good teachers are not afraid to risk appearing ridiculous; in fact, they often relish being thought of as "weird" and come to cherish being remembered in later years as eccentric. Eccentric – literally, off-centered – teachers knock students off their comfortable balance. When these students start to pick themselves up, they're in a position to learn what they need to know about how and where to place their own two feet.

This positive understanding of "disturb" also coincides with one conception of the role of the "student" as a person who learns through "inquiry," "investigation" and "discovery." You can see disturbance at work in those three words: inquisitive investigation toward possible discovery is often "messy" (and, it would seem that, definitionally, it must be).

It is the wise teacher who understands the significance of the words that students often use apologetically at the start of their response to a teacher's question: "I don't know but . . . ." In other words, "I don't know for a fact and I may be wrong, but I'm willing to risk failure by sharing some of these thoughts I'm having right now."

In the type of classroom where students and teacher actually *converse* on a regular basis – where questions flow back and forth among and between students and teacher – somebody, perhaps, but not necessarily, the teacher, might ask: "Why do so many of us in this room begin our contributions to a discussion with the words 'I don't know but'?" (And such follow-up questions as: "What might that 'I-don't-know-but' opening say about us individually?" and "What might it say about this classroom?")

But back to Miss Jean Brodie, who is often disturbing, always eccentric, and frequently ridiculous-looking in her embodiment of good teaching. The difficulty with a Jean Brodie is that her magnetism can be deeply "disturbing" in the highly negative meaning of that word. Miss Brodie's mission statement signature line – "Give me a girl at an impressionable age, and she is mine for life" – certainly captures in a hyperbolic way the daily demonstrated fact that teachers can make a difference in the lives of their students. Miss Brodie certainly does – for ill as well as for good. All of Miss Brodie's girls – especially the single one who ultimately betrays her – have their fates fashioned by this exceptional but also very flawed human being at a formative stage in their development.

To be an enlightening yet blinding role model and a master molder of minds is Miss Jean Brodie's "pedagogical persona" in her prime. She is Rick Dadier from *The Blackboard Jungle* taken to the nth degree. But Miss Brodie's prime years are also the years leading up to the Second World War, a time not without other individuals who take things to the extreme.

Though an inspiration to her cult-like disciples, the authoritative, imperious, at-times scary Miss Brodie is also a self-serving, self-deluded individual whose darker qualities cause her eventual betrayer to consider her former teacher "a born Fascist." How well does Jean Brodie know her "self"?

Is Miss Jean Brodie in her prime a dangerous teacher? How do we decide that? Where do we draw the line? And who does the "drawing"? Where does "in the place of the parents" become "replacing the parents" or "replacing society"? Where does it become "playing God"? These are difficult questions that require honest and extended reflection, and the readers of the novel *The Prime of Miss Jean Brodie* are not of one opinion on them. How could they be?

Nor may you be right now, or in your student teaching, or in your first-year of teaching, or at different points in your career thereafter. When many years later one of the more notable of the Brodie girls was asked by an interviewer who the major influence in her life was, she replied, "There was a Miss Jean Brodie in her prime." This woman was, in fact, the Brodie girl who was Miss Brodie's "assassinator." Wondrous, but maybe not so wonderful. Memorable, but also deeply troubling. Alive. Real. Hard to forget. However much you might try.

A commentary on circling the straight line

How different, then, are Jean Brodie and Malachy Dudgeon, the teacher in *The Dead School?* On the surface, Jean Brodie and Malachy Dudgeon may appear to be polar opposites: the North Pole of "in loco parentis" authority versus the South Pole of the "relaxed attitude" of not "really" being like a teacher. However, if you twist an imaginary straight line between these "poles" into a circle, the two teachers meet: both are failures at knowing themselves, their personas, and their schools. Both are kinds of "misfits."

As we said of Malachy Dudgeon, we can say of Jean Brodie: a teacher's persona does not operate in a vacuum; students within the context of a particular school occupy knowable space. And the teacher needs to "fit" into that space. Where do the teachers in the schools you know best fit in – and how? Which teachers from your experience are more like "Dudgy," or more like Miss Jean Brodie in her prime – and why?

Introduction to Sy Levin (the lone college instructor in this book)

For a different kind of "mis-fit," let's look at Sy Levin. Levin is a former New York City high school English teacher who goes west to teach composition at a California college in Bernard Malamud's novel *A New Life*.

Early on in the novel, Levin contemplates conduct that is both morally reprehensible and legally punishable: relating in a sexual way to a student in his class who has "made the first move." Up to this point in the story, Levin has paid Nadalee "no special attention." But then Nadalee, who is over the age of consent, visits Levin in his college campus office, ostensibly to ask about her composition grades. The two of them sit down to talk about her latest piece of course writing, and Nadalee leans her upper body against Levin's elbow enough times (by Levin's actual count, three) for Levin to conclude it was intentional. When Nadalee leaves the office "with not the vaguest sign of a blush on her," Levin finds himself glowing "as with high fever."

Levin's sexual yearnings for Nadalee read like the tortures of the damned: "Nadalee took on a private uniqueness, a nearness and dearness as though he were in love with her. Although he told himself he wasn't, she had in a sense offered love, and love was what Levin wanted. Though he tried diligently to cast her out of his thoughts, she sneaked back in with half her clothes off to incite him to undress the rest of her. He tried to figure out how to achieve an honorable relationship with the girl."

Levin wonders whether the ethics of his situation would be different if his and Nadalee's situation of place and time had been different: "if they were elsewhere in another season – if let's say, in the Catskills in July or August, he might with comparatively undisturbed conscience have taken a bit of what she offered. But here . . . she was his student and he her instructor, in loco parentis, practically a sacred trust. Levin determined to forget the girl, but his determination was affected by hers."

A commentary about sex between teacher and student? No, about "hands-on" teaching

What do we make of a college teacher whose pedagogical persona can be "affected" by an attractive student's interest in him? In other words, who do you think you are as a teacher – outside your classroom but inside your campus office, or across the boundary lines of another state? There are schools and school boards that seriously caution teachers against "laying a hand" on a student, and they're not referring to "corporal punishment," which is fairly widely condemned these days and usually illegal. "Touchy-feely" teaching is what they are talking about and usually how they talk about it.

As the sound of the term "touchy-feely" suggests, hugs, pats on the back, and the like (but what else is "the like"?) are frowned upon by some educators. However, when called something less "icky" than "touchy-feely," these kinds of physical contact between teacher and student are valued by still other educators as real, natural, human, valid, supportive, and caring. What are your feelings in this area? For you, what else is "the like"?

Instructor Levin engages in musings and mind games to find an iota of "honor" in a possible violation of "practically a sacred trust." Do you see Levin, as some readers do, as a self-defined "victim" whose achingly human attempts at blurring personal and professional personas are both sad and funny? Viewed this way, Levin's mind games are exquisitely particularized examples of situational ethics, rationalizations of fantasized behaviors that can be actualized "locationally" and "seasonally" – literally in another place at another time.

But back to our base in secondary education and to teacher Rick Dadier (as well as a colleague of his, Principal Small)

Sy Levin's personal and professional "mis-fit" may appear to some of us as perhaps sensational and sordid. Time now to re-visit Rick Dadier from Evan Hunter's novel *The Blackboard Jungle* – and also meet some of his veteran male colleagues – for a somewhat less dramatic divergence between a teacher's personal life and that teacher's professional pedagogical persona.

No matter what the pedagogical persona a teacher adopts, every persona causes a teacher's students to be cast in particularly delineated supporting roles. For one example, there is the teacher as the "lion-tamer" and the students as lions. ("But what happens to the best lion tamer," brand-new teacher Rick Dadier asks himself, "when he puts down his whip and his chair?")

Rick Dadier actually winds up adopting a well-known pedagogical persona that has been recommended to him by the school's principal, Mr. Small (the name says a lot – or at least enough). And it is a teacher identity quite different from Rick's own personal identity. (Rick's own wife would not recognize him.) As *The Blackboard Jungle* summarizes it:

> The first day was the all-important day. If you started with a mailed fist, you could later open that fist to reveal a velvet palm. If you let them step all over you at the beginning, there was no gaining control later. So, whereas a little Caesar was contrary to his usual somewhat easy-going manner, he recognized it as a necessity, and he felt no guilt. As Small had advised, he was showing the boys who was boss.

Your first day in front of your students is like opening night of a piece of performance art. Curtain up! By definition, you have only *one chance* to make a "first" impression on your students, and for Rick Dadier the curtain goes up on "little Caesar," a petty dictator. Rick's metaphor of a iron-mailed fist covering a velvet palm raises the question of what Rick's students' "second impression" will be of their teacher when Rick decides he can safely show his students "the real" Mr. Dadier in the classroom.

Will Rick's students be able – and willing – to trust the "truth" of this second impression, having already been "sucker-punched" by the iron-mailed fist from the first impression Rick made? It's problematic. *When* should teachers begin to "get real"? A recommendation: how about on Day 1 as soon as the classroom's "curtain" goes up and the spotlight shines on your teacher's persona?

Such metaphors as "curtain up" and "spotlight," by the way, are a reminder that good teaching, like good acting, is a prepared "performance" in a small "theater" before a specially invited "audience." Still, it is important to consider how little or much separation there should be between a teacher's character (actual basic personality) and a teacher's "character" (role being played). Actors, by the way, consider this question as well. If, like Rick, you are not a petty dictator in real life, why do you have to "play" one in the classroom? Who says you shouldn't smile in front of your students until at least three months into the school year?

By way of an answer, here's an example of a similar challenge to conventional wisdom from the history of American journalism: back in the 1960's, the very respectable yet perennial number two quality newspaper in New York City – *The New York Herald Tribune* – tried to lure readers away from the very reliable but fairly stodgy number one quality newspaper – *The New York Times*. How did the more modern-looking and contemporary-sounding *Trib* cut into the *Times*'s readership? The Trib started using a catchy new slogan that slyly but not all that subtly put down *The Times* (infamous as "the old gray lady" of 43rd Street) with the question: "Who says a good newspaper has to be dull?"

So, who says a good teacher has to be dull to the natural humor of any classroom? And yet a lot of veteran teachers still give "don't smile" advice to starting-out teachers. So, maybe the real question is: Who says their advice should be taken?

Smiling shows your students that you are as human as you find *them* to be, that you are "serious" about liking them, that the classroom is a real world place in which people are honest and genuine, and that teaching and learning are often fun endeavors. Smiling helps put the "joy" in joining together to learn. Last, but far from least, smiling is a great antidote when teachers – and students – need to lighten up and diffuse tension.

So, try entering the classroom smiling. Write the word "smiles" in the margin of a student's piece of writing when what that student wrote made you smile. Smiles are good-contagious. You can catch them from your students. They can catch them from you. No teacher has ever lost a class's respect from a smile.

Meet Lou Savoldi (veteran teacher, burned-out teacher)

The scene is the teachers' lunchroom in the novel *The Blackboard Jungle* and veteran teacher Lou Savoldi, in front of a captive audience of other teachers (in particular, novice Rick Dadier) is stating for the nth time and for all to hear his philosophy about the "correct" teacher persona. For Veteran Lou, these oft-repeated instances of cafeteria philosophizing (always exactly repeated, as dogma usually is) are always major mentoring moments for him.

But how does Lou's fatherly professional advice sit with his potential students of the craft of teaching? Well, as a person who might go into teaching, how do you feel about what teacher Lou Savoldi says?

> I'm like a man in a rainstorm. When the rain is coming down, I put on my raincoat. When I get home, I take off the coat and put it in the closet and forget all about it. That's what I do here. I become Mr. Savoldi the minute I step through the door to the school, and I'm Mr. Savoldi until 3:25 every day. Then I take off the Mr. Savoldi raincoat, and go home, and I become Lou again until the next morning. No worries that way.

A commentary on "Curtain Up!"

Lou Savoldi has split himself into two people with totally separate lives: there's the public persona of "Mr. Savoldi" and the private persona of "Lou." Whenever this teacher is in the "storm" of his school life, the "raincoat" of "Mr. Savoldi" completely protects the covered-up human being of "Lou." And when this man leaves school to go home, off comes his protective teacher persona and he is once again the untouched-by-his-students "Lou" – fully forgetful of any worries connected with being a teacher.

But returning to Lou's colleague Rick Dadier (student of teaching) and his musings on Mr. Chips (best known fictional teacher in the world)

To his credit, Rick, unlike Lou, doesn't "forget all about" his life as a teacher. In fact, that large part of his life is the subject of on-going self-evaluative conversations that Rick has with himself throughout *The Blackboard Jungle*. In one of the earliest of these "musings," Rick invokes the name of perhaps that most famous fictional teacher ever: Mr. Chips from the novel *Good-bye, Mr. Chips* by the British author James Hilton.

This particular self-evaluative conversation of Rick's begins with the notion that "whereas tough teachers were not always loved, they were always respected.

He was not particularly interested in being loved. Mr. Chips was a nice enough old man, but Rick was not ready to say good-by yet. He was interested in doing his job, and that job was teaching."

And Rick comes to the conclusion that "in a vocational school you had to be tough in order to teach. You had to be tough, or you never got the chance to teach. It was like administering a shot of penicillin to a squirming, protesting three-year-old. The three-year-old didn't know the penicillin was good for him. The doctor simply had to ignore the squirming and the protesting and jab the needle directly into the quivering buttocks."

So for Rick, it's goodbye and good riddance to Mr. Chips. However, for one thing, Rick is actually inaccurate and unfair in his implied characterization of Mr. Chips as "a nice enough old man" who was "particularly interested in being loved." In "fictional" truth, Mr. Chips, just like Rick, considered student obedience to be a necessary and essential foundation for his teaching. "Honor" (what Rick calls "respect") was "granted him" afterwards, and "love" from his students was bestowed only after his young, late-in-life bride, Kathie, had a "remarkable" *softening effect* on him. (Kathie tragically dies with their first child in childbirth within two years of their marriage.)

In fact, Mr. Chips (and it is in character that we do not know his first name) "assumed" on *his* first day of teaching a facial "scowl" in order to "cover" his inner nervousness. In addition, in his early years as a teacher Mr. Chips was a "dry and rather neutral sort of person; liked and thought well of by Brookfield in general, but not of the stuff that makes for great popularity or that stirs great affection." Only after his marriage, when Mr. Chips becomes the kind of teacher "who was kind without being soft" and "who understood them well enough, but not too much" does Mr. Chips become "beloved."

To create a straw man to knock down, Rick distorts Mr. Chips' true pedagogical persona in order to bolster his argument that "in a vocational school you had to be tough in order to teach." His disservice to a "kind without being soft" Mr. Chips does little to persuade us. Also, what are we to make of Rick's implication that students can – and should – only love a teacher in retrospect (the "one-day-way-in-the-future-you'll-thank-me" school of teaching, so, clearly, "today" is not going to be that day)?

A last point on this soul-searching of Rick's: just how apt is Rick's doctor/ penicillin, teacher/learning metaphor? Any good dictionary's definition of the verb "to educate" makes it clear that teachers are *not* engaged in "the filling in of an empty vessel" (the student) with all kinds of "stuff that is good for you." Nor are they consumed with writing on students' minds as if those minds were "blank slates" to be filled in. Instead, when good teachers "educate," they are literally engaged in "a leading out."

And concluding the chapter with Rick Dadier, the very first of our fictional teachers)

In an early scene in *The Blackboard Jungle*, Rick has his students working on that traditional opening day activity of filling out attendance cards. For those students who have come unprepared with any writing implement, Rick has thought to bring a supply of pencils from home. The scene shows in action and interaction the teacher persona that Rick has decided to adopt as a brand-new teacher.

When Rick makes an offer of pencils to anyone who is unprepared and needs one, one of the teenage students toward the back of the room (a husky boy named Sullivan) calls out, "I do, teach." Rick's immediate and angry reaction is to say, "Let's knock off this 'teach' business right now. My name is Mr. Dadier. You call me that, or you'll learn what extra homework is."

Rick's sudden fury surprises the class. As for Sullivan's response to Rick's threat of extra homework for any future violation, it's, "Sure, Mr. Dadier." Next, Rick says to the boy, "Come get your pencil." Watching as Sullivan rises from his seat "nonchalantly," Rick realizes that Sullivan is older than the other boys in this all-male class and sizes him up immediately "as a left-backer, a troublemaker, the kind Small had warned against."

Wearing a white tee shirt and tight dungarees, his hands shoved down into his back hip pockets, Sullivan strides to the front of the room, "taking the pencil gingerly from Rick's hand." Smiling, Sullivan says, "Thanks, teach."

"What's your name?" Rick asks, and the boy, smiling again (or still), responds, "Sullivan." (It is at this point in the narrative that we're told that Sullivan's hair "was red, and a spatter of freckles crossed the bridge of his nose. He had a pleasant smile, and pleasant green eyes.")

"How would you like to visit me after school is out today, Sullivan?" Rick asks, and the boy, still (or again) smiling answers, "I wouldn't." This teacher-student dialogue ends with Rick's saying, "Then learn how to use my name."

"Sure," Sullivan says, smiling "a broad smile" before he turns his back on Rick, "walking lazily to his seat at the rear of the room."

By the end of this incident, Rick feels he has "lost some ground in the encounter with Sullivan," which may also mean that he has lost some ground with the class. But what does it mean to Rick to have "lost some ground"? Rick's angry reaction to Sullivan's game-playing – "his sudden fury surprising the class" – shows us how seriously Rick takes both the philosophy and practice of "in loco parentis."

It's a given to Rick that Sullivan's teachers, like Sullivan's parents, deserve genuine respect. Yet, from the very beginning to the very end of the scene in the novel this young man's verbal language ("teach"), his body language (turning his back on Rick and "walking lazily to his seat at the rear of the room"), and his facial expressions ("a broad insolent smile") paint a picture of dismissive disrespect. Since Rick wants to see himself as a tough teacher, and tough teachers are "always respected," even the slightest disrespect or false "show" of respect on the part of a student would mean to Rick that he has not succeeded in hiding his vulnerable "easy-going nature" under a believable tough exterior.

Rick responds as we would expect someone working on a tough professional teacher persona to respond: "Let's knock off this 'teach' business right now. My name is Mr. Dadier. You'll call me that or you'll learn what extra homework is." (An unfortunate, yet logical, inference that many students even today make from this teacher tactic is that homework is, indeed, a kind of punishment, and additional "sentencing" will be meted out to fit the crime.)

Concluding the confrontation with Sullivan and laying the groundwork for a brief lecture Rick feels he needs to give in order to gain back lost ground with the entire class, Rick asks Sullivan, "How would you like to visit me after school is out today?" – to which, still smiling, the boy answers, "I wouldn't." Rick counters with, "Then learn how to use my name." Sullivan, in a "show" of respect, tellingly has the last word – the monosyllabic "Sure" as he smiles his insolent smile, turns his back on the teacher, and walks lazily back to his seat.

Rick's musings after the encounter with Sullivan – to which the entire class was witness – prompt him to decide to give the class a brief lecture. In his preparatory musings, Rick had remembered Bob Canning, an ed school grad in the class before Rick's who, like Rick, had also gone on to teach in a vocational school, but only to leave the job after five months.

Rick recalls that "Bob had allowed the boys to call him 'Bob,' a real nice friendly gesture. The boys had all just loved good old 'Bob.' The boys loved good old 'Bob' so much that they waited for him on his way to the subway one night, and rolled him and stabbed him down the length of his left arm. Good old bleeding 'Bob.'" The "pal persona," pedagogically. Rick has vowed to himself that he will not make the same mistake.

This is Rick's brief lecture:

> To begin with, as I've already told you, there'll be none of this "teach" stuff in my classroom. I'll call you by your names, and you'll call me by mine. Common courtesy. I've also told you that there will be no calling out. If you have anything to say, you raise your hand. You will not speak until I call on you. Is that clear?

The boys make no comment, and Rick takes their silence for understanding.

Apparently, Rick believes that within the confines of the student-teacher relationship, "common courtesy" (though it seems not that common in Rick's new school) would require his students to address him with the honorific "Mr." in front of his surname; at the same time, Rick finds nothing improper in addressing these adolescent boys directly by *only* their last names. On the other hand, in certain contemporary schools, teachers are encouraged by the administration to let their students call them by their given name. Know your school, and know whether you and its "culture" are a comfortable fit.

In *The Blackboard Jungle*, the clear implication from Rick's recollection of the story of Bob Canning is that allowing students to call you by your given name, as though you were their pal and, thus, not an authority figure like a parent ("in loco parentis"), is just asking for trouble – trouble like a pre-meditated physical attack and robbery. "Rick would not make the same mistake."

From the authoritative tone of Rick's lecture ("Is that clear?") and from such details as the hand-raising requirement and the no-calling-out rule, it *is* "clear" that Rick really means business. However, since "business" is a transaction that takes both a seller and a buyer, it seems problematic that Rick's students are "buying" quite yet. The sound of silence doesn't only or necessarily mean consent.

As we conclude this chapter that began with the question title "Who do you think *you* are in the classroom?", let's pointedly raise a subset of that larger question: practical questions about perspective, protocol, and procedure that you will find you will need to answer for yourself before you teach your first class in your first school:

- What "perspective" do you want your students to have when they look at you? (It might help you to note your reaction to Bob Canning's "mistake" and Rick's taking it as an object lesson.)
- How can a teacher be friendly with students in the classroom and in the school building without becoming their "pal"?
- What decisions have you made or might make on such classroom protocol and procedure issues as how you and your students address each other and whether students will need to be called on before they can make a contribution to whole class instruction? (It is not too soon to reflect on how you plan to address this issue of teacher and student "address" and what your ultimate decision says about how you see your persona and its impact on the teacher-student relationship; you'll need to know how you feel about Rick's belief that "if you have anything to say, you raise your hand. You will not speak until I call on you.")
- If being called "teach" is disrespectful because it can be seen as a "snippy" way of saying "teacher," then how about allowing your students to call you "teacher"? No? What if your students have difficulty pronouncing your surname?
- How will you arrange the seating of students in your classroom in order to reflect how you see yourself, how you see your students, and how you want them to see you as their teacher?
- Do you think it is possible for a teacher to be respected by a student without being liked? How does your thinking take into account this chapter's consideration of "persona"?

Finally, to end where we began: who exactly do *you* think you are in the classroom? What is the "fit" between your current or intended teacher persona and your "real self"?

Oh, you don't – or won't – have a teacher persona?

Think again.

3

Psychological games
students and teachers play

Teachers from four novels ask the perennial question: "Whose rules are these, anyway?"

Cast of Characters

E. R. Braithwaite, *from* <u>To Sir, With Love</u> *by E. R. Braithwaite, Great Britain, 1959*
Rick Dadier, *from* <u>The Blackboard Jungle</u> *by Evan Hunter, United States, 1954*
Malachy Dudgeon, *from* <u>The Dead School</u> *by Patrick McCabe, Ireland, 1995*
Thomas Gradgrind and the visiting supervising "gentleman," *from the classic novel* <u>Hard Times</u> *by Charles Dickens, Great Britain, 1854 (fictional teachers #14 and #15)*

Introduction to psychological games students and teachers play in the classroom

Nobody's perfect. When student teachers and first-and second-year teachers hear this remark (and they do) from colleagues and others, they often interpret it as a kind, but misguided, way of telling them, "You blew it!" But the absolute truth is that *no* teacher is perfect – not even the most highly successful teacher who is about to retire after decades of satisfactory and productive teaching. In fact, if that teacher actually thinks he or she has attained perfection, it is definitely time to retire.

Perfection exists in an ideal world, and last time anyone looked there were no job vacancies there (come on, job *vacancies* in an ideal world!). In the real world, the best you can hope for – and work toward – is to get better and better as the teacher you are, day after day after day. Recognizing your successes and failures and learning from *both* of them is a process that renews itself with every academic year. (Truth be told, with every dawn of a new teaching day.)

So now that the pressure to achieve ideal perfection has been lifted from your sagging shoulders, let's indulge ourselves for a moment in a fantasy of "Let's Pretend":

You miraculously find yourself in an ideal student learning environment, one so conducive to true teaching that you start having the nightmare all teachers eventually (sometimes, periodically) have. You may know the one: you're a fraud about to be found out and fired. Interesting thing about this dream: the students always remain hungry for knowledge and eager for learning opportunities in their pursuit of understanding and eventual wisdom. And, of course, you know in your soul that they are completely deserving of someone so much better than you as their teacher.

Back on earth, of course, students are far from ideal. Some of these real-life students actually choose to work harder at *not learning* than giving in and learning. Ignorance may not be bliss but it can be comfortable. And one of the major weapons students have in the fight to avoid being educated and remain ignorant is their skill at game-playing. Not the kind of game-playing involving videos and the Internet but the psychological kind that has been described by Dr. Eric Berne in his definitive study of relationship power plays, *Games People Play*.

Published early in the second half of the 20th century, *Games People Play* did not explicitly focus on the psychological interplay between students and teachers in the classroom. However, Berne's games are the prototypes for *the games you will find yourself the loser of – and your teaching the loser of – if you don't know how they work.*

A commentary on the ultimate goal of the games students play

In the classroom, students win these games whenever they have successfully *delayed* the kind of teaching and learning that *can* and *should* and *will* take place if students and teachers are on the same side (actually, when there are no sides). Why is stalling the teaching process the "object" of the game for the "side" we'll call Students? Simply put, in the real world of the classroom, too many students see learning as hard work: *if students can delay actual teaching, they can postpone the hard work of learning. (Students are right about that reality.) Let the lesson begin? No way! Let inertia reign – and let the games begin!*

As *Games People Play* fundamentally demonstrated, human beings play a variety of games in their social interactions with other human beings in order to gain influence or power in specific situations. As with all kinds of games, these human relationship games involve taking "sides," devising "strategy," and implementing "tactics." In the games students play in the classroom, the sides – as some students and some teachers see it – are already drawn (Students vs. Teacher); and the "delay teaching" objective is known to most students and readily discovered by teachers who "wise up." Competition occurs whenever Teacher plays along, and victory is determined by the brilliance of the opposing strategies and the skill of the players' tactics.

Not only must your side's tactics (individual "moves") be in the service of your strategy (overall game plan) but your "countermoves" (responses to your opponent's moves) must continually demonstrate an understanding of your opponent's operational strategy if you are to successfully overcome it and win the game. In too many contemporary classrooms, students and teachers often fall into the seductive habit of game playing – and every time this happens, true teaching and real learning get check-mated.

Game-playing advice given to novice teacher E. R. Braithwaite by a veteran colleague

In E. R. Braithwaite's novel *To Sir, With Love* ("based on a true story" of Braithwaite's experiences in his first year of teaching), brand-new teacher Braithwaite gets some early advice from a veteran colleague. The "veteran" teacher tells him: "Me, I was born around hereabouts and they know it, so I can give as good as I get. Don't take any guff from them . . . or they'll give you hell. Sit heavily on them at first; then, if they play ball, you can always ease up."

Hmm. As a soon-to-be or brand-new teacher, what do you think of this particular professional advice? How strongly do feel the way you do?

A commentary on why "giving as good as you get" is a bad strategy

The language of game-playing is so comfortably embedded in our day-to-day conversations that even this quickly and easily given piece of advice from veteran teacher to novice is replete with direct and indirect game references: "Give as good as you get." "Don't take any guff from them." "They'll give you hell." "Sit heavily on them at first." "Then, if they play ball . . . ." "You can always ease up."

Soon after being shown "the way," Braithwaite decides to assess his students' knowledge of "weights and measures" by asking them which ones they can identify. One of the male students, bypassing Braithwaite's hand-raising rule, calls out a response: "Yeah, I know. Like heavyweight, light-heavy, cruiserweight, middle, light bantam, fly-weight, feather weight." Author Braithwaite tell us that "the student held up both hands like a toddler in kindergarten and was playfully counting off on his fingers" and that when he finished, the class laughed and "at that he stood up and bowed to them with mock gravity."

Certainly the student's body language demonstrates a desire on his part to delay Braithwaite's assessment of his class's knowledge of weights and measures. With the grabbed-at spotlight on him, the student plays to an audience of his peers: he counts off on his fingers each "weight" from the unanticipated subject area of boxing and he acknowledges the approving laughter with a stand-up bow of "mock gravity." Not "smart" about the realm of weights and measures that Braithwaite was assessing, the student plays the "smart-aleck."

But what if the student had responded only verbally – and with no obvious or apparent attitude or tone? Technically (that is to say, strictly speaking), the boxing categories the student rattles off *are* measurements of "weights."

Even if the teacher were to infer an intention on the student's part to be "too clever by half," would you as a new teacher just meeting your students for the first time choose to respond in a negative way based on that inference? Need your reaction be anything more than an acknowledgment of the technical correctness of the student's seven correct boxing weights? Or, perhaps, a possible compliment for the student's unexpected right answer is in order – along with a reminder not to call out. Better still, you might consider the student's response to the class for the rest of the students to respond to and comment on.

So, just where is the line between "smart" and "smart-aleck" – and how carefully should teachers be looking for it? Braithwaite's actual reaction, it turns out, is to acknowledge *to himself* that the student's verbal response was "really very funny, and in another place, at another time, I, too, would have laughed as uproariously as the rest." However, Braithwaite also feels personally disrespected by what he sees as the student's playfully calculated opening move in a game – a "fighting" response in more ways than one.

"Are you interested in boxing?" Braithwaite asks the student in his opening "countermove" – and the game of "give as good as you get" is under way. "Well," Braithwaite continues, "if you have at least learned to apply the table [of weights and measures] in that limited respect, it cannot be said that you are altogether stupid . . . ."

Braithwaite's countermove is a poor one. His put-down of the student is an emotional *reaction*, not a professional *response*. Coming from the anger in his heart rather than from a considered idea in his head, Braithwaite's opening salvo is a tactic ungrounded in any carefully devised overall game plan or strategy; its origins are in Braithwaite's desire to "give as good as you get" by belittling the student. However, in all psychological game-playing between human beings, moves floating free of a foundational strategy can get picked off one by one by an opponent who knows what he's up to (his own strategy) and where he's going with it.

It is not surprising, then, that most of the other students in the class (appreciative spectators to the game) support the Student side with laughter: they see their fellow student as winning. Being a novice at the game that he has started to play (the game of "give as good as you get"), Braithwaite resorts to sarcasm, which, unlike verbal irony, is by definition "mean-spirited." Publicly shaming a student he barely knows in front of the student's peers, Braithwaite couples the backhanded compliment "you have at least learned to apply the table in that limited respect" with the zinger "it cannot be said that you are altogether stupid." By simply reacting without any overall strategy, Braithwaite is already losing this game badly – and he knows it.

The ever-recurring student game of "Resistance to a New Teacher"

So what should Braithwaite do now in order to save himself both professionally and personally? The author Braithwaite tells us that he knew that he "had to do something, anything, and quickly. They were challenging my authority, probably with no feeling of antipathy to myself, but merely to maintain a kind of established convention of resistance to a new teacher, watching closely for any sign of weakness or indecision . . . ."

Thinking that "a fight was what they wanted," Braithwaite decides to continue game-"boxing" with the class and give his new students the fight they want: "That's enough!" he shouts, his voice sharp and loud enough to cut off the class's laughter.

Braithwaite recognizes that the game "give as good as you get" is more specifically the game we can call, as he does, "Resistance to a New Teacher." No one has a copyright on this game, as you might well know from your own experiences in the classroom as a student or teacher.

A commentary on the game "Resistance to a New Teacher" as played out by E. R. Braithwaite and his students

The game "Resistance to a New Teacher" is a classic. Played by students around the world, it is not – it is critical to note – meant to be taken *personally* by a new teacher. These students don't know *you* long enough and well enough to be out to get *you*! (Of course, over time, students' games can be decidedly personal if a teacher's behavior is seen as *"you're* asking for it.") However, in the case of Braithwaite's classroom, the conventional game of "resistance to a new teacher" is being traditionally re-enacted to challenge and test his professional confidence in his own authority. For many teachers just starting out, this is a "rite of passage."

Responding to Braithwaite's authoritatively "sharp and loud" command of "that's enough!" the class does stop laughing; however, some students make the opposing move against Braithwaite of "not smiling now, but glaring angrily at me." Braithwaite even hears a few murmurs of cursing. Then the lunch bell rings, ending morning classes.

Lunchtime over, Braithwaite finds that his lessons pass "without incident, but unsatisfactorily." Lunchtime may be over, but the game isn't. Watching the class do its thing (its "strategy" unfolding to reveal itself to anyone really trying to figure out what is going on), Braithwaite immediately notices that "the children neither chatted nor laughed, nor in any way challenged my authority, but at the same time they were unco-operative."

Behavior problems? The students' behavior was no problem in the all-too-narrow but traditional conception of the term: "They listened to me, or did the tasks assigned to them, like automata. My attempts at pleasantries were received with a chilly lack of response, which indicated that my earlier remarks had got under their skin. Their silent watchfulness was getting under mine."

Although Braithwaite's "personal" moves in the game are now intentionally "pleasant," when his students react at all it is less like humans and more like robots: none of them "put themselves" into any of the "tasks" Braithwaite asks them to do. Because Braithwaite's students have taken *his* game-playing personally, Teacher and Student sides are at a standoff, with each under the other's skin. However, because these students are much more experienced at game-playing than he is and are foiling Braithwaite's objective, Teacher is losing the game.

Perhaps you have heard the term "classroom management" a couple of times (or more!) since you started to think about being a teacher. What Braithwaite *has achieved* in the game he got lured into is to "manage his classroom." This accomplishment, however, was at the expense of Braithwaite's truly teaching his students. Fundamentally "unco-operative," Braithwaite's students successfully forestall the kind of true teaching and real learning that Braithwaite hopes to accomplish.

Prospective and relatively new teachers often confuse classroom management with teaching. *They are not the same.* Being a teacher is about teaching other human beings – call them "the class." A "classroom," unlike those who inhabit it, is a place – not the people in it. Empty classrooms can be locked with a key; empty classes can be "unlocked" – that is, opened for teaching. Successful teachers rarely have "classroom management" issues because their managing of the classroom is an indirect *but natural* by-product of their successful teaching of the class. Poor teachers may learn, right away or eventually, how to manage a classroom. But they remain poor teachers.

A critical reminder before we take a look at a few other games teachers and students play

It is vital to remember that unless you as a prospective or new teacher clearly understand what the winning any of these classroom games actually consists of, you will not be able to accurately analyze the strategy and tactics of each side. Failing that, you can never be confident about who has won and who has lost. Maybe there is no loser, depending on how the "winning" side has won the game.

And think about this: if, on the Student side, the meaning, purpose, and objective of any classroom game, as we commented early in this chapter, is to *delay* the kind of true teaching and real learning that *can* and *should* and *will take place* when students and teachers are on the same side (when there are no sides!), then "winning" (for all) would be whatever it takes, in a humane way, to quickly end the game, to get going with teaching and learning, and to keep from falling into this delaying trap again. If together you and your students openly explore these "rules," there'll be no game that can be "rigged" and education will be the big winner.

A shout-out to fictional teacher Rick Dadier (appearing for the third chapter in a row)

If you have ever been on the Teacher end of a game we can call "Me?" (or "Who, Me?"), the following brief dialogue from Evan Hunter's novel *The Blackboard Jungle* will sound familiar. A little bit into teacher Rick Dadier's first meeting with his class at the all-boys vocational high school Manual Trades, Rick notices that the room is somewhat stuffy. Rick could say something like *"Would someone open a window in here"* and risk "a mad scramble to the windows," but Rick knows from his education courses how to do this kind of thing "according to the book": you choose one student.

Rick clearly points to a male student sitting up front near his desk and asks: "What's your name?" The boy looks frightened, "as if he had been accused of something he hadn't done" and responds, "Me?"

Rick no doubt nods his head affirmatively as he answers, "Yes, what's your name?" And the boy ends the exchange with his surname: "Dover."

A few minutes later, Rick directly asks another male student to collect the attendance-taking cards the students have been busy filling out. As this second boy is "picking up the cards dutifully," Rick interrupts him to ask *his* name, and the boy answers, "Me?"

A commentary on the game "Me?" in <u>The Blackboard Jungle</u>

Since there is absolutely no doubt in these two instances about who is being addressed, the question "Me?" is, in fact, the game "Me?" However, because this is Rick Dadier's first day on the job, it will take him a little while to realize the real meaning of this game *as it is played in his school*. Rick muses that the answer "irritated him a little, but that was because he did not yet know 'Me?' was a standard answer at Manual Trades High School, where a boy always presupposed his own guilt even if he were completely innocent of any misdemeanor." Is it thus in schools you are familiar with?

When teachers ask a question, it's important that they quickly assess that the question has been understood with the same meaning and in the same spirit that it was asked. Experience shows that it can take some time for this practice to become habitual for new teachers. Until then, a teacher's wanting to learn a student's name may be heard by some students as the opening to an interrogation that ends with "guilty as charged."

The brief return of Malachy Dudgeon (the "good-as-dead" teacher in a "dead school")

In Patrick McCabe's novel *The Dead School*, the game of "Who, Me?" or "Me?" has the more respectful-sounding (and thus, perhaps, more infuriating) label of "Me, Sir?" It is well into the academic year and Irish parochial school teacher Malachy Dudgeon has come to believe that his nemesis, student Stephen Webb, is "trying his best to destroy the class." One morning, as he "unzipped his briefcase and eyeballed at the class as they filed into their seats," Malalchy tells himself that "Well by God let him try any of his tricks this morning and we'll see how far he'll get."

Of course in the game of "Me, Sir?" that Malachy then gets sucked into with Stephen Webb, the reader also gets to see "how far" Malachy gets. In fact, Malachy does so poorly in the game that it comes as no surprise to everyone, including Malachy, that he is not rehired at the end of the school year. In the opening move of the game, Malachy "barks" at Stephen, "Take your hands out of your pockets! Do you hear me?"

Of course, Stephen responds with, "Me, sir?" Now, watch how the game is staged by Stephen and Malachy:

> **Malachy** (snapping): "Yes, sir – you sir! Stand up when I'm talking to you!" (Of course, Stephen stands up; ah, but, "real slow, to drive you mad! And then that stupid, sickly sweet voice. And the big innocent face with its angelic kiss curl falling down over his stupid big eyes.")
> **Malachy**: "Take your hands out of your pockets I told you!"
> **Stephen**: "Sir, my hands aren't in my pockets"
> **Malachy** (grinning): "I see. Not in your pockets."
> **Stephen** (twiddling his fingers): "No, sir."
> **Malachy** (laughing): "Of course they're not. Sure how would they be in your pockets? God bless us, Stephen, sure a good boy like you would never put your hands in your pockets now would you?"
> **Stephen** (smiling, and dropping his eyelids): "No, sir."

Malachy (thinking to himself as he hears one of the other boys chuckle
    behind his hands): "Very well. Chuckle. I'll deal with you in my own
    good time."

A commentary on the game "Me, Sir?" in <u>The Dead School</u>

This seemingly pre-ordained sequence of moves is then exactly repeated by
Malachy and Stephen around the issue of whether Stephen has been laughing
all this time during their back-and-forth exchange: "You're going to tell me you
weren't laughing?" asks Malachy, noting, predictably, that the same other student is
again chuckling behind his hands during round two of moves and counter-moves.

The game ends with Malachy's saying to Stephen, "You really do think you
have an answer for everything, don't you, Stephen?" Stephen responds (not
surprisingly), "No, sir." Malachy counters with, "Oh but you do, sir."

Trying for the last word and the end of the game Stephen says, "No, sir," while
it is Malachy, spreading his fingers on the desk, who does get the last word: "Sit
down please." Malachy is grinning right at Stephen as he ends the game, trying
hard to not laugh out loud.

Clearly, Malachy thinks that Stephen has lost the game. Malachy muses: "The
little upstart really thought he could best him. He really did. What an idiot."
Shaking his head, Malachy almost says out loud to Stephen: "I mean just how
stupid can you get!"

The game of "No, sir" is finally over and Malachy is smugly confident he has
won it. But has he? What's been going on here?

Or maybe the question should be: all this time, what teaching has been
going on? What has the class been learning? Is that what the teacher planned on
teaching as today's lesson? "No, sir!"

Still, teacher Malachy Dudgeon thinks he has won the game of "no, sir" – or
won at least something. But what?

Teacher is convinced his side has "best" the "little upstart" of a student. But
this is Student's game being played by Student's rules: the game "Me, Sir?" has
morphed into "No, Sir" (which is the same as "Not Me, Sir"). Student's side is so
in control of the game that it "tricks" Teacher's side into always repeating what is
fundamentally Teacher's only (and losing) countermove.

The result: for as long as Teacher continues to play the game (it begins to
come to an end with the tactical move "Sit down please"), Teacher will repeatedly
feed into the opposition's strategy. This game can go on forever – or at least until
the bell rings ending the period. If the objective of the game "No, Sir" is to waste
time and forestall teaching and learning, then its objective has been achieved;
the "delays" continue like posted domestic flight departures in an overburdened
American airport: the result is that education gets delayed and delayed and

delayed, and ultimately gets canceled. Nobody boards the plane, the flight never takes off, and all the students in what should be a first-class educational situation get left behind in their education.

Speaking of being "left behind," the school "superintendent" and one-room schoolhouse we meet next – from a classic British novel – is a frighteningly similar nineteenth-century version of too much of the late twentieth-century's American educational policy that there be "No Child Left Behind."

Introduction (and, full disclosure) of a teacher and supervisor you really don't want to meet – Thomas Gradgrind (he grinds students down)

Set in the mid-nineteenth century, Charles Dickens's novel *Hard Times* has great fun mocking the horrific educational theories of Thomas Gradgrind during one of Gradgrind's visits to a "model" school to observe its workings and to quiz its students. (The "outrageousness" of Dickens's prose style is meant to startle the reader into feeling genuine "outrage" at the educational system he depicts.)

Thomas Gradgrind is a fanatic in his belief that education should consist of "gallons of facts" being poured "full to the brim" into little boys and girls. To test the learning of his "little vessels," Gradgrind and an accompanying visitor referred to only as "the gentleman" proceed to conduct "oral quizzings" for which there are only three kinds of answer: right, wrong, and no answer (silence on the part of the interrogated student). Regrettably, too much of this is strikingly like an oral version of the much-debated use of standardized testing in the United States today.

A commentary on "imagine that!"

Perhaps you have witnessed classrooms that are essentially if not exactly like this kind of "grinding" down of a young person's capacity to wonder, to imagine, and to think critically and creatively – game-playing at its classic best. As a soon-to-be or new teacher, you will want to assess just what it is that the "girls and boys" side of the game learns as the pupils "play" along, as well as what the teacher side of the game intended to teach and actually thought it was teaching. And, you might find it reassuring to pull out all the stops and quote no less a teacher than Albert Einstein, who stated: "While knowledge defines all we currently know and understand, imagination points to all we might yet discover and create."

The sad truth behind the satire of Charles Dickens

Charles Dickens's use of broad satire to ridicule his century's version of "No Child Left Behind" may be difficult for some of us to read because of its heavy-handedness. But it should definitely be difficult *for all of us* to read because of the sad truths behind Dickens's overt ridicule.

The game of "No Mind Left, Be Child" (oops, "No Child Left Behind"), begins in an early chapter of *Hard Times* when the visitor accompanying superintendent Thomas Gradgrind to a "model" school asks of "the boys and girls" whether they would wallpaper a room with representations, that is, depictions, of horses. Immediately after a short pause, "one half the children cried in chorus, 'Yes, Sir!' Upon which the other half, seeing in the gentleman's face that Yes was wrong, cried out in chorus, 'No, Sir!' – *as is customary in these examinations* (italics mine)."

"Of course, No," the visitor responds, definitively (there is *no question about it*). He then continues, "Why wouldn't you?" When a "corpulent slow boy" ventures to answer that he wouldn't paper a room at all (*a question about it!*), explaining that, instead, he would paint it, the know-it-all visitor insists, "You *must* paper it (italics Dickens)." To which Superintendent Gradgrind adds his pound sterling of authority: "You must paper it whether you like it or not. Don't tell *us* you wouldn't paper it (italics Dickens). What do you mean, boy?"

The visitor then explains why the boy shouldn't mean what he's said when it comes to why you should never wallpaper a room with representations of horses: "Do you ever see horses?" he answers with a rhetorical question (and, thus, by definition, not meant to be answered back), "horses walking up and down the sides of rooms in reality – in fact? Do you?"

"Yes, Sir!" calls out one half of the room. "No, Sir" comes from the other. "Of course, No," replies the gentleman, with "an indignant look at the wrong half." And he adds, by way of unchallengeable explanation and logic: "Why, then, you are not to see anywhere what you don't see in fact; you are not to have anywhere what you don't have in fact. What is called Taste is only another name for Fact." And Thomas Gradgrind nods his approbation.

A commentary on the games of "Murder, He Smote" and "Murder, He Rote"

The game is now well under way as Gradgrind's educational theories are demonstrated in practice – a game that Dickens might call "Murder, He Smote," since it graphically depicts what Dickens calls the "murdering" of innocent young children by the *systematic* destruction of their "imaginations" and their sense of "wonder." If this is what Gradgrind wants taught and tested, then taught and tested it has been.

And if this is Gradgrind's instructional objective, then he is frighteningly close to achieving it. No wonder (it's not allowed!) that the accompanying "gentleman" is overjoyed when he can eventually point out to "girl number twenty," Cecilia (Sissy) Jupe: "That's it! You are never to fancy," to wonder. (Dickens characterizes the visitor during his involvement with the challenging and free-spirited Sissy as "smiling in the calm strength of his knowledge.")

Sissy was one of just a few pupils who had said "yes" (not the hoped-for answer, and, thus, the wrong answer!) to the gentleman's second question (same game as "representations of horses" on wallpaper): in this go-round, the issue is whether you would ever carpet a room with "representations of flowers on it." The correct answer is, *of course* (italics mine), "No," and the reason is, well, by now you get what the reason is, unless you're not into playing the game of "Murder, He Rote (sic)."

Sissy's non-factual reason, which she blushes to admit, is: "If you please, Sir, I am very fond of flowers." And she concludes, "It wouldn't hurt them, Sir. They wouldn't crush and wither, if you please, Sir. They would be the pictures of what was very pleasant, and I would fancy . . . ." But, cued by Sissy's use of the idea and word "fancy," the visitor interrupts: "Ay, ay, ay! But you must never fancy," cries the gentleman, "quite elated" by coming so happily to his point. "That's it! You are never to fancy."

And Gradgrind solemnly repeats: "You are not, Cecilia Jupe, to do anything of that kind."

"Fact, fact, fact!" said the gentleman. And "fact, fact, fact!" repeated Thomas Gradgrind.

A commentary on some educational hope in the "answers" of students like Sissy Jupe and in the teacher art of thoughtful questioning

However, despite the day-in-and-day-out "grind" of this model school's efforts, *Hard Times* does give a glimpse of educational hope to its readers through the answers and explanations of Sissy Jupe and the "corpulent slow boy with a wheezy manner of breathing": they are the only two pupils (but at least there are two of them) who show any resistance to their school's stultifying instructional program.

Sissy not only insists on her "fancies" but can provide supporting reasons along logical and realistic lines: why *not* have flowers in your carpet's design if it's flowers that you're "fond of," as she challenges the visitor's disbelief that Sissy would, actually, put tables and chairs upon carpets "and have people walking all over them with heavy boots." Sissy quite logically points out that they're not real flowers that could get crushed or would wither by the weight of people walking on them or by furniture resting on them!

Good grief, Sissy might say today, these are representations of things, not the actual things themselves! Haven't any of you so-called educators ever taken a course in semantics! If knowledge is power, don't you know that you can't "hurt" symbols! Certainly the so-called "corpulent slow boy" makes a lot of sense when he realistically relates that the reason *he* would not "paper a room with representations of horses" is that he would *prefer* to paint his walls rather than to wallpaper them.

Teachers for whom there is "only one right answer to my question and that is the answer that *I* have in my head right now" have no patience with such students. The boy's "right answer" is *all* that Teacher needs, and wants, to hear; *no one* will ever know whether any two "wrongs" in the student's head – the student's reasoning process – "made" the "right" answer that came out of the student's mouth.

And if the answer out of the student's mouth is *wrong* (or at least not the answer Teacher is expecting), well, we're *certainly* not interested in hearing aloud the process that led to an error or mistake! In fact, we're not listening. Please just regurgitate all the right answers you've been fed (rote, rote, rote); that is "the one needful thing," which is the full title of this early chapter of *Hard Times*. (A teacher that appears in this same chapter is satirically called by Dickens "Mr. McChoakumchild" because he both philosophically and practically "chokes" children full with as many *right answers* as he possibly can.)

Good teachers today recognize that it is exactly from hearing aloud how students arrive at their "right" – and their "wrong" – answers that educators are given a major teaching and learning opportunity: to have students "think about thinking" and then to teach them how to work at "thinking better." This is teaching the process of "critical thinking" at its very best and its most natural.

Experienced teachers know that sometimes what sounds like the most bizarre "wrong" answer can turn out to be a truly great insight (one, in point of fact, that the teacher did not anticipate); however, teachers and students can only have this experience if a classroom's conversation regularly consists of follow-up questions that require students to *think aloud about the thinking process*. Here are a few variously worded examples of this technique:

- "Hmm, interesting" or "that's intriguing," so, what makes (or made) you think that?
- Where do you see that?
- Where does it say that? Where did it tell you that?
- So, where does it imply that, then?
- Can you find specific words or details that support your point? How about any images or examples?
- Where did you get that idea from?
- Forget about whether your answer is "right" or "wrong" or neither, would you please share with all of us what you are basing it on?
- What led you to form that particular opinion?
- Why do you think you have that reaction?

- Why not have a go at sharing with us the thinking that brought you to that conclusion?
- Can you convince us to change our minds and adopt your point of view, or do we have to take your word for it?
- What would it take to convince you to change your mind?
- Did you walk into the classroom already believing this, or did we just have a specific experience that put the idea in your head?

Experienced teachers also know to listen in their own lessons and those of their colleagues for such small but powerful words as: *why?*, *how?*, *why not?*, *how come?*, *so?*, *how so?*, *explain your thinking*, *your reasons?*, *because*, *thus*, *therefore*.

Class "discussions" like the ones you *want* to have across the curriculum in your subject classroom – discussions that are real back-and-forth conversations involving thinking and feeling, reasoning *and* imagining ("what if?") – this is not at all what is wanted by the Gradgrinds of the educational world, whatever the century they live and work in – and create teacher and student achievement standards for.

For these "Gradgrinds," most classroom *teacher-to-student* talk is but "an oral quiz"; regular instruction (outside of so-called "group work") largely consists of the teacher's constant and all-pervasive drumming into the class's collective mind (no individualization here!) a set of conventionally accepted right answers to a pre-determined set of fact-based questions – in short (in all senses of the term), the answers that are always marked "correct" on rote-memory and standardized tests.

A direct consequence of this educational philosophy and practice is that little or no time is teacher-planned anymore for *full-class* student-to-student talk and interaction of much interest, consequence, or significance. All eyes are meant to be on the teacher at the front of the room.

Hard to believe? Check your colleagues' so-called "lesson" plans (and your own!) for proof that the craft (and, at some future time, the art) of thoughtful questioning – the very essence of good teaching – is largely missing; much too often, "lesson" plans nowadays look "less" like plans and more than a little like a *schedule* of four or more "activities" for forty-five minutes of purported "instruction."

How has this limited aspect of planning and teaching (two separate yet fundamentally connected creative acts – and both difficult to pull off without hard work) come to represent the essence of planning and teaching in so many American schools in recent decades?

Fundamentally, it would seem from observational evidence that students are being egregiously short-changed because they are assumed to have – hello! – short attention spans. However, as Linda Loman says in that justly famous line of dialogue in Arthur Miller's play *Death of a Salesman*, "Attention must be paid."

But by whom? And to whom?

By teachers to all students. And by students to other students.

It is this kind of "collective attention" that makes students into a "class." And, as has been said elsewhere in these pages, a classroom is not the same "species" as a class. The time cannot come too soon for the classroom to once again be both "house" and "home" to this kind of "collaborative learning" for the class's teacher and each and every student present for a full period of full-class instruction.

Until this day is *made to arrive* in our nation's schools, day-to-day instruction will remain synonymous with ongoing oral testing (and look and sound exactly like it; check it out!). Perhaps we should at least be truthful about what we called the process and go back to what it was actually termed in the nineteenth century: "Training." It's certainly a game both teachers and students can play comfortably and well.

A corroborating side note

In recent years, high school students' challenges to "incorrect answers" on the traditionally required college PSATs and SATs increasingly make the national news whenever "The College Board" is forced to publicly admit that a student's "wrong" answer was actually "right," in fact (*in fact!*) more insightfully "right" than the officially sanctioned to-be-bubbled-in "right answer."

The student game of "Psyching Out the Teacher"

Ironically (so, of course, purposefully on Dickens part), *Hard Times* offers a glimmer of hope for true education from the way three of the depicted pupils play a psychological game different from "Regurgitate the Right Answer." We might label this other game "Psyching Out the Teacher." You've no doubt seen variants of it in classrooms you've been in as a high school and college student, a student teacher, an observer of teachers, and (maybe) a teacher yourself.

These three mid-nineteenth-century students have, at least, learned the tactic (move or counter-move in any game) of watching a teacher's facial expressions for context clues to the desired answer: "seeing in the gentleman's face that the Yes was wrong"; and "the gentleman, smiling in the calm strength of knowledge" that he has, knows he has, and believes a particular pupil ("girl number twenty") shares with him.

And even though these young students, in fact, make the mistake of thinking that a discerned pattern will always hold ("there being a general conviction by this time that 'No, sir!' was always the right answer to this gentleman"), we should credit them for observing, making connections, seeing possible patterns, making inferences, and reasonably drawing possible conclusions to the point of conviction. These are all "mindful," not "mindless," activities – and "*mindful*" is exactly what we should want students – and teachers – to be at all times (not only in *hard times*). Just as we would want all plans to be created with care ("careful," now) because what is the use – the practical use! – of a plan that is thrown together "carelessly"?

Games teachers play with their students

We'll end this chapter by giving teachers *their* due: some games that teachers *initiate* with their students. One game that some starting-out teachers in the United States have been especially susceptible to play since around the 1960's might be called "With-It."

In the game of "With It," Teacher works extremely hard to please Students by impressing the class with how young and "with it" he or she is when it comes to either popular culture preferences, or the use of street "lingo," or an expert command of state-of-the-art technology and "special effects" in the classroom. Each of Teacher's moves in this game is calculated to enhance the impression of how "cool," "with it," or "one of us" Teacher is.

A commentary on the teacher games of "With It" and "Show Me You're Interested Even If You're Not"

However (and of course), that's the problem with this game: if your strategy is to be so popular with your students that you adopt an "I'm-one-of-you" persona as their teacher, your students will let you win. As with all games, we need to ask what the objective is; in "With-It," the objective is the same for both Teacher and Students: your relinquishing of your role as their teacher.

Student teachers and first-year teachers are particularly prone to be seduced by themselves and their students into an ongoing (the whole term!) game of "With-It." This is often because in the early stages of learning by doing, such teachers usually obsess over the question "How am I doing?" This question, too, can evolve into its own kind of game that teachers play either with colleagues or themselves (a mental solitaire).

However, since the suspected truth of how you are doing at this early point in your teaching career may hurt your professional pride, there are, understandably, times you may not want to truly ask the question or play this particular game.

You might even, on a particularly "teeth-pulling" day, resort to the teacher game of "Show Me You're Interested Even If You're Not."

More than one education major over the years has shared an experience involving a co-operating teacher's observation of that student teacher's teaching almost identical to this actual example:

> As one of her daily observations of my teaching performance, my co-operating teacher noticed that there was a moment during my lesson when I was "losing it." What she heard, I realized, was my attempt to erase the looks of boredom written across many students' faces by saying, "Even if you're not interested, look like it, or express interest through alert body behavior." I was affirming students' negative attitude towards reading a book they would like to be finished with before Christmas!

Like this perceptive student teacher, all teachers need to ask themselves how much of their adopted persona and which parts of any games they play in the classroom can be traced to a lack of confidence in their personal qualities, their "training" as a teacher, or their current lesson-planning and lesson-teaching skills. To peel back these labels and probe, you will want to reflect on such questions as:

- How do you as a teacher know what it is you want to and need to teach in your subject area?
- What are *your* desired outcomes? How do you know that the "how" of your teaching will get you to the "what" of your students' learning?
- How do you know moment to moment (ongoing assessment), lesson to lesson, week to week, unit to unit, course to course, essay to essay, formal test to formal test, professional evaluation to professional evaluation that you are teaching what you intended to teach and are actually achieving your aims, instructional goals, objectives (you name it; actually, it probably has already been named for you – see "educational jargon")?
- What feedback do you get from your students moment to moment (ongoing assessment), lesson to lesson, week to week, unit to unit, essay to essay, formal test to formal test, course to course?
- What have your students learned from you that you didn't set out to teach them? If you don't know, how come? How do you feel about that? How can you find out?
- What feedback do you get from co-operating teachers, colleagues, field supervisors, mentors, bosses? How valuable is this feedback to you? Why is that? Are you succeeding in internalizing their specific recommendations and suggestions?
- How are your personal strengths and weaknesses (Chapter 1: "know thyself") a factor in your making the constructive (non-judgmental, supportive) criticism you receive a structured part of your journey to become the best possible teacher you can be?

- How have you made self-criticism (insightful, non-over-the-top) a regular part of your journey to become the best possible teacher you can be?
- What classroom psychological games do you play or allow your students to play that forestall or undercut teaching and learning? How can you end them so that both you and your students win the game?

As you explore these questions year after year of your teaching career, try to keep both your ears and all of your mind open. Don't be made nervous by the unexpected (it's inevitable!) when it occurs in your classroom; instead, embrace the surprises: every "problem" can rightly be seen as an "opportunity in disguise" for good teaching and real learning. Try to be "anxious" in the sense of "eager" – not in the sense of "nervous."

Of course, always seek to be a student of your own teaching experiences; welcome what students can tell you and teach you through their *feedback* about your instruction. You can probably on your own (try it) come up with a solid list of examples of how students provide teachers with positive feedback.

To give you a head-start prompt on the other side of the teaching/learning ledger, it's important to note that boredom, and restlessness, and sleeping in class, and frequent or regular requests for the bathroom pass, and cursing, and back-talking, and major game-playing, and disruptive behavior on the part of one or more individuals are just a few examples of feedback about both your teaching and about teaching in general.

There is no war, battle, or competition between you and your students: *together* you are a work in progress. Talk both process and progress with your classes, and teach them how to distinguish between process and product.

Talk with your students – and teach your students – about the nature and varying styles of teaching as well as the nature and individualized styles of learning. Then teach your students how to teach one another – and how to teach you to be better at your chosen profession.

Talk with your students as individuals, talk with them when you join them in small groups, talk with them as much as you can as part of full-class instruction.

Talk. And let the lessons – not the games – begin!

4

Discipline problems?
Who has discipline problems?

*F*ive fictional teachers model why some real-life teachers have no discipline problems to speak of – with the very same students who are wreaking havoc in the room of the teacher next door

Cast of Characters

Veteran teacher Mr. Jackson, *from* <u>The Longest Journey</u> *by E. M. Forster, Great Britain, 1922 (fictional teacher #16)*

Rick Dadier, *from* <u>The Blackboard Jungle</u> *by Evan Hunter, United States, 1954*

Josef Blau, *from* <u>The Class</u> *by Hermann Ungar, Germany, 1927 (English translation by Mike Mitchell, 2003) (fictional teacher #17)*

Ms. Hawthorne, *from* <u>Freshman Focus</u> *by Carla R. Sarratt, United States, 2007 (fictional teacher #18)*

E. R. Braithwaite, *from* <u>To Sir, With Love</u> *by E.R. Braithwaite, Great Britain, 1959*

Introduction to "discipline problems? Who has discipline problems?"

In E. M. Forster's *The Longest Journey* (the good news for you is that the title refers *not* to a career in teaching but to the institution of marriage), Mr. Jackson is a veteran teacher of the Sixth Form – and, the novel's readers are told, he is "the only first-class intellect" in Sawston School other than the headmaster. Since many of you are probably familiar with the term "classroom management" or can guess at its intended meaning, you might want to visualize Mr. Jackson's class of students through the lens of that seemingly euphemistic term.

Forster informs his readers that Mr. Jackson "could not or rather would not, keep order. He told his form that if it chose to listen to him, it would learn; if it

57

didn't, it wouldn't. One half listened. The other half made paper frogs, and bored holes in the raised map of Italy with their penknives."

Forster concludes his description of Mr. Jackson's classroom with the educational philosophy underpinning this veteran teacher's way of dealing with the reality before him:

> When the penknives gritted he punished them with undue severity, and then forgot to make them show the punishments up (sic). Yet out of this chaos two facts emerged. Half the boys got scholarships at the University, and some of them – including several of the paper-frog sort – remained friends with him throughout their lives.

A commentary on "chaos" in the classroom

When you reflected on Mr. Jackson's style of classroom management, did you at all take into account the "yet" comment about the "two facts" that "emerged"? Perhaps you wondered about a possible *implication* that these facts are the "results" of Mr. Jackson's preference for allowing the natural course of human events to occur in his classroom without any input from him. Logically, these so-called "ends" might not have resulted from their so-called "means": sequence isn't the same as causality; there certainly is no *research evidence* (assessment, anyone?) that they did. But even if we could show causality, would these ends justify those means?

More fundamentally, what should we think of a teacher who leaves the entire semester's conduct of the class completely up to the students after giving them just one "let the buyer beware" warning about educational consequences? Today's supervisors of teachers would certainly be concerned about the effect of the conduct of the uninvolved students on those who were trying to pay attention. Not only would these supervisors also have something to say about the need to teach students skilled ways to discipline themselves but they would make specific recommendations about monitoring and assessing students' practice and progress (including the importance of following through on threatened punishments) and about when and how to re-teach self-discipline skills.

Still, there is no denying the wisdom underlying the one action Mr. Jackson takes before he descends into inaction on the question of discipline: he does tell his class (as so many other teachers have told theirs) that whether to learn or not is ultimately the student's decision. It's true that no teacher can *make* a student learn against the student's desire or will; however, the simple "take-it-or-leave it" basis on which Mr. Jackson presents the option does not speak well (actually, at all) for the importance of getting an education.

Teachers can, and should, "speak up" for the value of an education, and they should motivate students to learn and teach students how to go about it (in fact, practicing self-discipline is one of the ways). "Making" students learn is not good pedagogy. Teaching them how to is. Mr. Jackson understands neither his job nor the seriousness of his action's consequences. This is more than oblivious teaching; this is irresponsible teaching.

In Evan Hunter's novel *The Blackboard Jungle*, Rick Dadier, as a prospective New York City high school English teacher, is in the process of "acing" his job interview. Rick truly wants to be a responsible teacher. Not unnaturally, the thought of possible "chaos" in the classroom is on his mind. The chair, deciding to end the interview with a job offer, collegially asks Rick, "Any questions?"

Rick responds: "Just one, sir," but hesitates just a moment before beginning his question. Then he says, "The discipline problem here. Is it . . . ?" Rick doesn't get to finish the question. The chair's eyes tighten, and he says quickly, "There is no discipline problem here. I'll look for you on Friday." The chair immediately rises from his seat and takes Rick's hand. Rick, too, rises from his seat, but "uncertainly." End of meeting. No further discussion. Actually, no discussion to begin with.

Yet the "here" of the chair's response is the very school characterized in the novel's threatening title as a "blackboard jungle." (This academic "jungle" was originally branded as *The Tiger Pit* in author Evan Hunter's earlier and shorter unpublished version of the story.)

Five formulas for establishing discipline among the "animals"

No matter whether North Manual Trades is seen by its teachers as a "pit" or a "jungle," different members of the faculty have developed a variety of "formulas" for establishing discipline among the students they think of as "animals." Author Evan Hunter gives these discipline approaches such cutesy titles as Clobbering, Slobbering, Slumbering . . . .

Clobbering

As he periodically explains to his colleagues in the teachers' lunchroom, physical education teacher and coach Captain Schaefer is a prime believer that one should: "Clobber the bastards. It's the only thing that works. What do you think happens at home when they open their yaps? Pow, right on the noggin. That's the only language they understand." Clobbering is considered "in loco parentis" at its best by this high school teacher.

Even a non-physical teacher like Rick Dadier can understand that a teacher's urge to clobber a teenage student may often be present not too far below the teacher's professional surface – particularly in the context of such a highly physical domain as a school's body-oriented gymnasium or athletic field. However, Rick believes he could not "in all honesty, picture himself doing that" – even though "it was sometimes more difficult not to strike than it would have been to strike, and the consequences be damned."

Slobbering

Another method of discipline at North Manual Trades was Slobbering. It worked particularly well when used by a female teacher because it coupled a teacher's "I'm-touched-to-the-quick" facial expression with her verbal complaint about the ingratitude of her all-boys' class. The Slobberer whines, "After all I've done for you, you give me this treatment" – and, perhaps because of the boys' innate chivalry, a bunch of hoodlums is made to feel like heels. (The most common form of male Slobbering, one that might appeal to a group of boys' sense of fraternal spirit with their teacher, would sound like this male teacher's plea: "Come on, fellows, give me a break. I'm just a poor slob trying to do a job, that's all.")

Slumbering

The Slumberer, in sharp contrast to the Clobberer and the Slobberer, treats the whole question of discipline as a non-existent problem: he chooses to ignore the situation totally and proceeds to teach from the start of the period to the ending bell – and if no one pays any attention to what he is teaching, well, that's just too bad. He's there to teach, they're there to learn, and as long as he's done what he's being paid to do, he's done his job. Just as some people sleep-walk, the Slumberer sleep-teaches.

Rumbling

While the Slumberer knows there is no discipline whatsoever in his classroom and is okay with that, the Rumbler is a teacher exactly like the Slumberer except for one thing: the Rumbler invariably complains about the lack of school discipline at the end of each sleep-teaching day. He complains to his wife, to the department chair, to the principal, even. The Rumbler can even be heard complaining to himself when there is no one else around to listen. Never blaming himself, the Rumbler especially blames last year's Slumberers who allowed such a "shocking" disciplinary problem to develop.

Fumbling

The Fumbler is a teacher who simply does not know what to do about discipline. (Rick early on in *The Blackboard Jungle* considers himself a Fumbler.) Fumblers keep trying – first this way, then that way – hoping that someday they will miraculously hit upon the "cure-all" for the discipline problem. Although some Fumblers eventually work out a solution for themselves, many Fumblers become proponents of either clobbering, or slobbering, or slumbering, or rumbling.

A commentary on why it might actually be accurate for a school's leadership to say, "There is no discipline problem here"

Questions about discipline, whichever the school and whatever its academic standing, are invariably raised in one form or another by job applicants and newly hired teachers. In fact, Rick makes this question his *only* question during his job interview with the English chair. (If *you* get to ask only one question during your job interview, what would it be? Why is that?)

Let's also note at the start of this commentary that Rick seems to suggest *at the start of his question* that he believes there *is* a discipline problem at this particular school. "The discipline problem here . . ." are the words Rick uses as a lead-in to a question he plans on asking about the nature and extent of an assumed discipline problem at North Manual Trades High School. It's quite possible, however, that what Rick means by the phrase "the discipline problem" is *the subject of discipline in general.* After all, no school – no matter how successful – is without its problem students.

We can give Rick the benefit of this doubt and still make the point that for some people in the general population, and for some of Rick's colleagues at North Manual Trades, there seems to be an underlying assumption that schools in urban areas are *filled* with "problem students." Perhaps this is the reason that English Chair Stanley is depicted in the novel as abruptly protective of his school's reputation: when Rick raises the subject of "the discipline problem," Mr. Stanley's eyes tighten and he quickly cuts Rick off with: "There is no discipline problem here"; Chair Stanley then *immediately* restates his job offer to Rick and *ends the interview* ("I'll look for you on Friday"), leaving Rick with nothing more to do or say but rise from his seat "uncertainly" and say, "Yes, sir; thank you, sir."

A similar "given" about middle school students (suburban and exurban as well as urban) is that, first, their young age and, later, their "raging hormones" are the problem. Tellingly, 22-year-old Dan Brown subtitles his 2007 memoir of his first year teaching a "dumping ground" class of 4th-graders in a Bronx, NY, *elementary* school ("The Great Expectations School" of Brown's title): "a rookie year in the new blackboard jungle."

Rick Dadier, in the "original" *The Blackboard Jungle* may have "heard pretty good reports" about North Manual Trades, but has he done any pre-interview research? We don't know. Here's what we *do* know: all starting-out teachers need to be aware of any assumptions they may have about a school's "student body" and the implications these assumptions have for their teacher persona and for their planning and teaching.

Although some teachers find it extremely difficult to teach students with psychological or emotional or family problems, others do not; in fact, they thrive on it. Whichever teacher you are, all of your students deserve understanding and the full resources of the school to address their needs. *Doing nothing more than saying* that these students "*are* problems" is to brand them and dismiss them. *And to say* that an entire group of students "*is* a problem class" *and to stop there* is to ignore the human mix of individuals that shakes and stirs a class. The solution to the so-called "problem class" is to work with, and on, the "elements" producing the wrong kind of "chemistry," not simply to bemoan the poor chemistry.

We all recognize that there are students who *have* problems but do not *cause* problems. We also know that there are students with problems who *make* problems for some, though not all, of their teachers. When they do this, they are also *making problems for other students and entire classes.* But teachers must also look at their personas, their content material, and their planning and teaching if we are to more fully understand why certain students are wreaking havoc in one classroom while working at learning in the room of the teacher next door.

As to an entire school's having "a discipline problem," that's a whole other *matter* – a matter of *the school's* leadership, its instructional philosophy, its staffing methods, its managing and monitoring of its programs – and we need to find all of this out. These are large matters, big deals.

Rick Dadier of *The Blackboard Jungle* seems to understand these distinctions: during his successful job interview, Rick went out of his way to tell the interviewer that as a student teacher he had had a good experience in another New York City vocational high school. In contrast, some of his new colleagues have concluded that it stands to reason that because *they* have discipline problems, everybody in their vocational high school does. But this is the kind of "reasoning" we know as rationalizing.

It's not too hard to fall into the rationalization trap when the reason you're reluctant to evaluate your own teaching is the fear that you might already be "the best possible teacher you can be" – and your best is not all that good. But, like Mr. Jackson in *The Longest Journey*, this is being irresponsible; if you don't "own" your weaknesses, you can't take possession of and develop your strengths.

Meet Josef Blau and his Czech class in <u>The Class</u>

An extreme, yet instructive, example of a teacher's need to "know thyself" as the foundation for real understanding of how discipline operates in a classroom can be found in the novel *The Class* by Hermann Ungar, first published in Germany in 1927 and translated into English by Mike Mitchell in 2003.

Josef Blau is a high school teacher in a small Czech town; he himself comes from a poor family but in his first teaching assignment Blau gets a school in a district of the town where the well-to-do part of the population live. "At the very start of *The Class*, Blau is shown to be beyond neurotic in his fear of his class of eighteen fourteen-year-old male students. The opening lines of Chapter 1 *almost* say it all: "He knew that the boys were watching his every move; the slightest chink in his armour could expose him to disaster."

Fighting "with all the means at his disposal" to manage his class and maintain discipline, Blau, though himself not cruel by nature, is resigned to appearing "cruel" because he is convinced that otherwise everything will be lost – most specifically, his job:

> There were examples he had heard of from which he had learnt that leniency and indulgence were not the way to keep boys in check. That had led to the downfall of other teachers, for once the restraint of discipline had gone, everything would be in vain . . . . There would be no respite once they sensed, even for a moment, that their mocking laughter would pursue him when he was forced to flee, humiliated, head bowed, deprived of his livelihood.

Because Blau was "aware of the freedom of movement and self-confidence a well-to-do background gave a person," he was afraid that this was where "the first chinks in his armour might appear. He could feel the boys' eyes scrutinizing his movements and his clothes."

In response, Blau stood facing the class, unmoving, his back against the wall: "his eye held them, individually and as a whole. He knew that he must not miss the least flicker of a smile, however secretive, on one of the faces turned towards him. It could be the smile of arrogance and the beginning of the revolt. If he saw it in time, he could extinguish it with a look. He could also find some excuse to punish it. The most important thing was to keep concentrating for every moment of the lesson on the goal of not letting discipline slacken under any circumstances."

Unlike other teachers, Blau would never walk up and down the classroom. Such behavior as going from motionlessness to motion, Blau was convinced, "broke the tension," "blurred the boundary between authority and the uniform block of those subject to it," changed the system from "rigid" to "flexible" – in effect, "released forces he could not control."

In addition, Blau's own fixed position "offered less chance of exposing his movements to the boys' scrutiny than would be the case if he were walking up and down." Likewise, having students, as was usual, go to the chalkboard to write their answers would break the straight line of sight from them to him and from him to them, creating a new, disruptive grouping. Never from the moment he entered the classroom was Josef's Blau's back exposed to the class: he positioned himself in such a way that "the wall shielded his back from being seen . . . . He stayed there, facing the boys, until the end of the lesson."

A commentary on "don't anybody move!"

Obsessively self-conscious about his origins, his undernourished physical appearance, and the impoverished look and quality of his clothes, new teacher Josef Blau is insecure to the pathological point of believing that his well-to-do students have a secret but barely hidden contempt for him based on social class. Blau's objective as a teacher is to prevent open rebellion, chaos, and the otherwise certain loss of his job. And Blau is convinced that only by imposing a rigidly regulated discipline on his class can he achieve his objective. This pedagogical paranoia produces near paralysis: Blau suffers from a kind of "motion" (and "emotion") sickness as he literally maneuvers and positions his body in the classroom so that his back is never to his students and his eye is always fixed on them.

This relationship between "emotion" and "motion" in the classroom was also evident – though less surrealistically! – in the novel *The Blackboard Jungle* when we watched author Evan Hunter turn the spotlight on such disciplinarians as the Clobberer, the Slobberer, the Slumberer, the Rumbler, and the Fumbler. Besides their all having catchy labels, these five disciplinary personas (Rick Dadier calls some of them "degrading") are also alike in that they deal with discipline not as a subject to be addressed proactively but as a problem to be solved after the fact.

Not one of these five categories captures an approach that is "problem preventive," that actually sets out to "establish" *a disciplined class of students.* Even the Fumbler's attempts to do this are more "hit or miss" than well planned. The field of education needs to be doing more than responding to "sickness"; it needs to be promoting "wellness," an orientation already under way in the field of medicine.

Just what do we mean by "discipline," anyway?

One way to re-orient our approach to discipline in the direction of "wellness" is to go back and take a look at some original meanings of the word "discipline." First off, you probably know that "discipline" is also a synonym for "the subject matter under study" and that it is related to the word "disciple." So what does it mean to be a "disciple" (in both sacred and secular terms)?

Disciples are individuals who eagerly embrace the teachings of someone with wisdom to share. They are the devoted followers of a master teacher; "disciple," in fact, comes from "discipulus," Latin for "student" or "pupil." Disciples are motivated to discipline themselves to the rigors of truly learning the subject under study. At some point, these learnings, for convenience sake, are grouped together as the concepts and workings of particular branches of knowledge – such subjects for study as English and math and biology and so on. The various disciplines.

Headmaster Florian in E. R. Braithwaite's novel *To Sir, With Love* captures a bit of both the "subject matter" meaning of discipline and its derivation from "disciple" when, seven months into the school year, he perceptively comments on Braithwaite's progress as a teacher: "I think you were setting too much store by quick results. After all, we are not concerned here merely with academic effort; our idea is to teach them to live with one another, sharing, caring, helping. It's not easy for them," these rigors of true learning.

As an education major writes in the student teacher's professional journal:

> Class control is a balancing act that takes great skill and experience (or, in some cases, a natural gift). As student teachers, we run into these students who disrupt or avoid work. Many teachers take a hard approach and insist on drastic consequences, harsh ones because "the teacher must never be weak and most always be dominant." As a student teacher I have asked about "control" in the classroom and I have experimented with different styles (thanks, students, for letting me "practice" my skills on you). I have found that a relaxed, light-hearted demeanor works best for me, but that I should also be clear and objective and fair about standards in the class.

A commentary on discipline from Day 1

If discipline is something that is *established* among a community of learners (and that community includes the teacher), then it is most effectively established on Day One. Teachers who spend the *entire* first session of the semester on administrative and clerical mandates – registering students and keeping them busy filling out all kinds of paperwork, creating a fixed-in-stone seating plan, lecturing on all the rules and regulations until the bell rings – such teachers actually miss the foundation opportunity to create lasting discipline by teaching "something" of substance to introduce and begin the term's work and motivate student interest in it.

By not sending the message that every class moment is important and that real teaching and learning gets priority every day the class meets, these teachers may actually be setting the kind of tone that allows discipline problems to occur. How teachers allot and juggle the time demands of teaching students and conducting "school business" within an all-too-brief class period speaks volumes about what these teachers' priorities are, how they see their pedagogical persona, and how passionate they are about teaching and about their subject matter.

Since the true "business" of a class is teaching and learning, teachers worried about discipline problems down the road should examine the timing and sequencing of what they do, conventionally or habitually, during the first meeting of a class. Not only is there a need to handle administrative mandates more efficiently but it is best to locate them toward the middle or end of the first class period (or save some of them for part of the work of Day Two) after real teaching has taken place and "grabbed the class."

Getting the journey of the course off to this educationally sound start is exactly the way to prevent that time immemorial scenario generically known as "That Night at Home after the First Day of School":

> **Parent to child**: "How was your first day of school? What did you learn?"
> **Student to parent**: "Bor-i-i-n-n-g! I didn't learn anything. All we did was fill out the same old forms in every class and hear all about rules and regulations."

Why would any young person want to return for Day Two?

Introduction to the "fair" discipline of fictional teacher Carla Sarratt's contemporary class

In Carla R. Sarratt's 2007 novel *Freshman Focus*, set in Charlotte, North Carolina, it is Day One and student Mia Floyd gives voice to this feeling of boredom at the very start of Ms. Hawthorne's freshman English class. Calling out loud from the back of the room, Mia wants to know from Ms. Hawthorne "as she prepared to greet her students": "Are you about to give us the rules again?" (Well, are ya? She was.) There are a number of emotional tones Mia's line can be read aloud in – and none of them is positive.

Wisely and immediately learning from student feedback, Ms. Hawthorne proposes postponing to the class's second session any going over of rules and procedures and invites the students, instead, to today "play a game to become better acquainted with each other . . . . Does that sound fair to everyone?"

A commentary on "smiles all around the room"

The game is "Find Someone Who"; it has "fifteen statements and the object of the game is to find someone in the room who fits that statement." We're told that there were "smiles all around the room. Students began to relax in the less tense environment" and that one of the male students thought to himself that "this could easily become his favorite class if it were not for those five books that Ms. Hawthorne was having them read."

Before we end this chapter

In a later chapter of this book, we will feature two extended case studies of how a misunderstanding of the concept of discipline and its relationship to teaching and learning can lead to disaster in the classroom; therefore, in anticipation, we conclude this chapter with a case study in microcosm of two teachers of classes that are geographically an ocean apart but that educationally could be in adjoining classrooms.

New York City vocational school teacher Rick Dadier of *The Blackboard Jungle* and East London "ghetto" teacher E. R. Braithwaite of *To Sir, With Love* both "fumble" to reach out to and connect with their students. Take a moment to compare and contrast these two teachers – Dadier and Braithwaite: what would you say is the key insight they come to about the teaching/learning dynamic as they strive to complete their first year of teaching?

Brand-new teacher Rick Dadier in <u>The Blackboard Jungle</u>

He spent the next week observing his classes. He taught, or tried to teach, while he was observing, but he was really stalling for time, trying to learn in one week all the things he'd never been taught. On this Monday of October 19th, he did not know if he was any closer to teaching the kids. But he had some ideas now, just a few ideas . . . . He sensed that the beginning of the teaching process had to come from the kids themselves. He knew, in fact, that there could be no beginning in this school unless the kids desired it.

Standing up there in front of the room and throwing facts at them was a waste of time, until they realized there could be no teaching and no learning unless there was a give and take. And rather than spend all his giving time giving, and hoping they would be taking, he'd decided to let them do a little giving, let them do all the giving in fact, until this sense of mutual exchange became a habit.

Brand-new teacher E. R. Braithwaite in <u>To Sir, With Love</u>

Next morning I had an idea. It was nothing clear cut, merely speculative, but I considered it all the way to school. Then, after assembly, as soon as they were quiet I waded in. This might be a bit rough, I thought, but here goes.

"I am your teacher, and I think it right and proper that I should let you know something of my plans for this class." I tried to pitch my voice into its most informally pleasant register. "We're going to talk, you and I, but we'll be reasonable with each other. I would like you to listen to me without interrupting in any way, and when I'm through any one of you may say your piece without interruption from me." I was making it up as I went along and watching them; at the least sign that it wouldn't work I'd drop it, fast.

They were interested, in spite of themselves; even the husky blasé Denham was leaning forward on his desk watching me.

"My business here is to teach you, and I shall do my best to make my teaching as interesting as possible. If at any time I say anything which you do not understand or with which you do not agree, I would be pleased if you would let me know."

A commentary on "a less tense environment"

Like the more experienced Ms. Hawthorne in *Freshman Focus*, these two starting-out teachers, Dadier and Braithwaite, have come to understand the importance of immediately creating a "less tense environment" in which teaching and learning can take root. And, like Ms. Hawthorne, their understanding includes a teacher's learning something about his or her students' personalities, interests, and likes and dislikes on the very first day of class. As the Chinese proverb puts it: "a journey of a thousand miles begins with one step." And it goes without saying that starting-out teachers are likely to be worried that that first step is not a misstep.

A commentary on "it goes without saying"

It goes without saying that the "it" in "it goes without saying" is always something generally thought of as obvious, common sense, "the given." The truth is, however, that those things we say go without saying inevitably need to be said – in fact, *will be said right after that introductory phrase*. They don't go without "saying."

So it goes without saying that you teach the students you have – not the students you want to have, not the students you think you deserve to have. Discipline problems *generally* arise from a "disconnect" between a teacher's style and methodology on the one hand and the learning styles and needs of that teacher's students on the other. Experienced teachers like Ms. Hawthorne in *Freshman Focus* – open-eyed, open-eared, and open-minded – meet their students where they are ("Are you about to give us the rules again?") so that teacher and students can begin the journey together. Disciplinary "disconnects" are repaired as soon as they are encountered.

For discipline problems that are of "another kind," it goes without saying that, well, here goes: there obviously are discipline "cases" that are not part of this pattern. However, these are all of a "kind" – for these are the students who bring their emotional, psychological, physical, personal, and familial problems with them into the classroom – any classroom, perhaps most classrooms. Not necessarily every day but most days, clearly often enough for them to be in need of the specialized resources that may be available *to you for them.*

You know who the people are who constitute these resources: parents (yes, parents!), deans, guidance counselors, peer mediators, conflict resolution and anger management specialists, community social workers, family counselors, special education evaluators, after-school-activities coordinators – the whole panoply of professionals that American schools are increasingly making use of but far too many schools have been "left behind" without. These people can help you, the teacher, help your individual students. A caution: don't reach for a "referral" as a first response: you've got some skills in many of these areas that you can employ as a first resort. But don't wait too long to call on these other people as a "second resort," which comes way before "a last resort."

It goes without saying that, in general, these people know what they're doing and that it is not truly in the service of the student for you, only minimally trained in these specialized areas, to *substitute* your "best shot" at help for their professional and personal expertise.

Yes, be a caring "first responder," but know and respect your limitations. Just like a doctor, your first obligation as a teacher is to "do no harm." Clearly, you are the very person who will be best able to identify when "a discipline case" is *incidental.* These cases arise out of *specific* problems that are no less dramatic (or traumatic) and can happen to the best of students – either at home with their parents, siblings, or their own children; in their part-time jobs; or in their personal life, including their love life.

As teachers, we need to be sensitive to unexpected deviations from an individual student's normal behavior, and we should arrange to meet *privately* with that student or with a small group of similarly affected students to see whether we personally can be of help before we help by referral.

Let's say, then, that we should approach the five types of cleverly labeled disciplinarians from Evan Hunter's *The Blackboard Jungle* as traps to avoid, as negative role models: don't do what I do, don't say what I say, don't be the persona that I am. It's more than likely that some of these disciplinary categories strike you as, at best, dated or at worst, clichéd. To single out the first category – the Clobberer – for example: certainly there are very few school systems today that would not frown on corporal punishment if they haven't, in fact, already made it illegal. Still, there is that little town in Texas that recently authorized people who are both licensed gun holders and licensed teachers to bring their firearms to school for possible retaliatory use in extreme cases of student violence against a school's staff and student body.

Perhaps some of the other "-ers" of Evan Hunter's disciplinary personas – the Slobberer, the Slumberer, the Rumbler – strike you as peculiar. Perhaps not. Do any of them reflect your high school experiences with teachers? Do one or two "ring" true or at least plausible? Whatever and whichever, let those that do "be a lesson to you."

It goes without saying.

5

Are you in the right place? Knowing the kind of school you want – and learning how to go about getting a position there

A couple of teachers new to this book – plus three "veteran" fictional teachers – demonstrate the importance of having a very specific idea of what your "ideal" school would consist of; even better, they point the way toward doing what it takes to find your ideal school or a "reasonable" real-world facsimile

Cast of Characters

Sy Levin, *from* <u>A New Life</u> *by Bernard Malamud, United States, 1961*

Rick Dadier, *from* <u>The Blackboard Jungle</u> *by Evan Hunter, United States, 1954*

E. R. Braithwaite, *from* <u>To Sir, With Love</u> *by E. R. Braithwaite, Great Britain, 1959*

Tom Mason, *from* <u>Schooled in Murder</u> *by Mark Richard Zubro, United States, 2008 (fictional teacher #19)*

Justin Hearnfeld, *from* <u>The Misadventures of Justin Hearnfeld</u> *by Dan Elish, United States, 2008 (fictional teacher #20)*

An introduction to "knowing the kind of school you want – and learning how to go about getting a position there"

It turns out that the previous chapter's defining problem – that of "the discipline problem in your school" – has as one of its underlying assumptions the very real and natural fear that you as a prospective teacher might wind up teaching in the "wrong school" – for you.

If you think there could NOT possibly be a "wrong" school for you given how difficult it is for new teachers to find a teaching job these days (you'll take anything, anything!), you might be tempted to skip this chapter. Before you yield to that temptation (particularly if you are skeptical of those introductory words in bold type about "knowing the kind of the school you want – and learning how to go about getting a position there"), please read at least four more paragraphs (the next four; they're in italics to tempt you on) before you skim or skip the remaining pages to get quickly to Chapter 6.

Do you think you're going to be told here that the job situation is going to change real soon? No way. The job situation is not going to change any time soon – and, besides, even if it were to, that would not be a strong enough reason to persuade you to read this chapter now rather than later or not at all.

No one is going to come to your home to try to force you to read this chapter because it is truly important to your knowing yourself as a teacher that you have an idea in your mind right now of what kind of school you would love to teach in. No one is going to ring your doorbell in order to tell you that – but THAT is the reason: it is truly, truly important to your knowing yourself as a teacher that you have an idea – pretty much right now – of what kind of school you would love to teach in.

Student teachers who request that their site schools be changed know exactly why they want out of a particular school. Certified teachers in their very first school who find themselves wondering whether they can survive the semester without being "certified" in another way know exactly why they are so unhappy in their job. Experienced teachers in the throes of burnout . . . well, you get the picture.

So, would it hurt you to know from reading this chapter right now "the what" and "the why" of your ideal school even though it probably won't be the first school you get to teach in . . . but it could be the last? Your ideal school should be the basis for the comparisons you make among all the actual schools you get to experience. Late in this chapter (go ahead, peek), you will come upon a list of questions you can ask of your first potential school so that you will not wind up being a fatalist about where you work Day 1, Year 1. Thanks for listening.

If you're still with us, meet Sy Levin

"Are you in the right place?" asks the question in this chapter's title – figuratively. If you think it would be hard to imagine a teacher's being any more than figuratively in the wrong place, Bernard Malamud, the author of the novel *A New Life*, thinks otherwise. Sy Levin is literally in the wrong place.

It's the summer of 1950. Sy Levin is a 30-year-old New York City *high school* English teacher of two years' experience who has come to believe that his "manifest destiny" is to teach *literature* in a *liberal arts college* out west.

Are you in the right place? Knowing the kind of school you want –
and learning how to go about getting a position there

73

Following some correspondence between him and a Dr. Gerald Gilley, who is in charge of his college's hiring process, Levin believes he has been hired, sight unseen, for the job he wants, in the kind of school he wants, in the part of the United States in which he wants to be a teacher. Ideal.

Actually, unbelievable. For as Levin learns on his arrival in town, the job Dr. Gilley has selected him for is to teach composition (not literature) in the local *college specializing in vocational subjects.* Levin is in the wrong place! (For Levin.) Literally – and figuratively.

Sy Levin and Dr. Gilly first meet when Dr. Gilley picks a clueless Levin up at the train station, and in the course of their first conversation, Levin happens to express his opinion that America's liberal arts colleges are "making a serious mistake" if they're starting to consider favoring vocational, that is to say, trade, subjects over the liberal arts.

Levin's out-of-sync comment and Dr. Gilly's thoughtful response clue the novel's readers into Levin's probable acceptance-of-job-offer mistake: "All I can say, Sy, is I hope you didn't write to the wrong place when you wrote us for a job. Some people get us mixed up with our . . . adjunct, and vice versa."

Levin thinks, "Holy mackerel" and comes to the conclusion that since he had written for a job at both Cascadia colleges – the liberal arts one and the vocational one – he must have gotten confused about which was which since the liberal arts college had, in fact, turned his job application down. The career result is that Levin winds up in what for him was not "the right place" to be both personally and professionally.

Yet the it's-too-late-now circumstances force Levin to tell Dr. Gilley the exact opposite of what Levin is feeling at the moment, and so he ends their conversation with "I'm glad to be teaching here." (It is possible that Levin may continue to feel for a lifetime of moments that he is teaching in the "wrong place." It has been known to happen, as some veteran teachers can tell you.)

It makes you wonder what kind of pre-interview job application preparation a prospective teacher needs to do in order to lessen the likelihood that your first teaching position will be really "the wrong place" for you philosophically. So, let's wonder together.

A commentary on a job offer – take it or take it?

Sy Levin *is* glad to be teaching any aspect of English anywhere out west: his job options were not optimal. But you? Will you be so grateful to be offered any teaching position anywhere that "if *they* want you, *you* want them"?

If your professional situation is not quite that desperate, your job interview will be important not only for your answers to their questions but also for the questions you ask in order to learn as much as you can about their school. It is not inconceivable that it may be *you* who winds up doing the rejecting because you realize that this school is not for you.

To improve your interviewing skills, one of the most proactive things you can do is have one or more knowledgeable individuals conduct mock interviews with you. The great thing about mock interviews is that they enable you to discover and practice your strengths, discover and eliminate your weaknesses, and build up your personal and professional sense of self.

In preparation for a mock interview, try, if you can, to co-create with your pretend-interviewers likely *generic* questions that would allow you to address how your special qualities, particular background, and remarkable experiences are "a perfect match" to what you already know a given school is looking for. Take your mock interviews seriously. Never "walk through" or "wing" them: good mock interviewers always evaluate, judge, and give feedback on such important intangibles as your professional attitude, your energy level, your ease and self-confidence, your passion, your sense of humor – even your facial expressions (eye contact, smiles) and body language.

A *warning*

Some people find mock interviews more difficult than real ones because they don't want to look bad in front of someone they know fairly well. Just as it is important to choose your mock interviewer carefully, it is important to get over this fear of embarrassment: a key idea behind mock interviews is for you to come across "bad enough" during these practice sessions so you can learn from your mistakes. Mock interviews are only "mock" in the sense of "let's pretend," not in the sense of "poke fun at."

Sy Levin's never having had a job interview (real, let alone mock) was a big mistake. But let's leave Levin happy to be at any college out west and return to the city, subject, and teaching level that Levin left back east: New York City, English, high school.

Rick Dadier sets his sights on a teaching position

Rick Dadier, the teacher in Evan Hunter's novel *The Blackboard Jungle*, is about to interview for an open English teacher's position at North Manual Trades High School in New York City. Rick's wife is pregnant with their first child; he "fervently" wants to teach; and, financially, Rick badly needs a job.

If you were Rick, you might be thinking: Is this non-academic, vocational school the "right place" for me, even though I really could use the job and, so far, this is the only one I have a shot at?

Are you in the right place? Knowing the kind of school you want –
and learning how to go about getting a position there

75

However, still "you" as Rick, you might simultaneously be wondering what your "ideal" school would be like, sensing you might know it when you see it. Yet, Rick being Rick, you would probably also feel challenged to create "a recipe" for your "ideal" school, coming up with the precise amounts of carefully specified ingredients.

If you're not Rick, however, you might be thinking, Why do I have to rise to this challenge? Or, you might consider this whole train of thought much too philosophical and unrealistically academic.

Rick's interview with English Chair Stanley at North Manual Trades High School runs four pages in *The Blackboard Jungle* and is worth checking out as a set piece for the well handling of its several turning points; indeed, the interview is a beautifully choreographed back-and-forth "game" played by two near-masters, and, as a consequence, it cannot truly be captured even in extensive quotation.

The interview begins with Chair Stanley's asking Rick to "sit down, won't you?" and climaxes with Rick's not quite realizing that he's been offered the position when Chair Stanley says, "Can you be here Friday for an Organizational Meeting, Mr. Dadier?"

A commentary on the two-way conversation called "a job interview"

Literally, an interview of any kind means that for two people there is "a seeing of each other." In Rick Dadier's interview with English Department Chair Stanley – and Stanley's interview with Rick – the two men both see each other and try to see into each other (as in a friendly game of checkers). Rick is critically aware of the importance of content and process in an interview: having observed and overheard Stanley's interview of the previous candidate (don't ever count on finding yourself in a similar and, actually, unprofessional, scenario!), Rick uses his "mental notes" on that interviewee's (and Stanley's) weaknesses and strengths so that there will not need to be a "next candidate" after him.

Stanley's first interview question of Rick is "Why do you want to teach here?" and it is *the* question all starting-out teachers should expect to be asked and be prepared to answer – fully, yet concisely – at any point in all interviews. Rick's truthful, yet strategic, answer is "I have to teach in a vocational school." (The reason Rick has to is, at that time, the New York City Board of Education required new teachers with an emergency license – which is what Rick has – to teach one year in a *vocational* high school in order to get their license validated.)

As the individual in charge of hiring for his department, Stanley would, in all probability, know about this citywide requirement; nevertheless, Stanley, when he hears Rick's response to the opening question of "Why do you want to teach here?" doesn't come back with something like "Right, so you have an emergency license, then." Instead, probing to get to know this interviewee better, Stanley instead asks,

"Would you rather teach in another type of school?" Rick is skillful to pick up on Stanley's "suspicious" tone, smiling "a bit tremulously" as he gives himself time to consider a somewhat risky answer: "Sir, I would rather teach at Princeton . . . but so would a lot of other people."

Not everyone would have risked these particular words and this tone with so little prior knowledge of the kind of person the interviewer is. Rick's response is a calculated decision – just as is his scrupulous attention to his diction, enunciation, and pronunciation during the course of the interview right after he has picked up on Stanley's careful pronunciation of "student" as "styu-dent."

With respect to the "I would rather teach at Princeton . . . ." comment, from Stanley's quick smile Rick correctly infers that "he'd hit the right spot," that the gamble had paid off, and he "could take whatever Stanley had to offer now." He feels in charge of the interview and can barely contain himself in anticipation of Stanley's next question. (He is confident without coming across as cocky.)

How big or slight a gamble do you feel Rick has taken here? You can test your confidence in your own feelings with "what if" questions like: what if instead of using the name of a prestigious Ivy League college, Rick had used the name of a hard-to-get-into, admissions-based high school like the prestigious Townsend Harris High School in Flushing, Queens, New York? Or what if he had used *a neighborhood academic high school with a merely okay reputation*? "What if" questions can also be instructive when you analyze your mock interviews or a just-completed actual interview; they help you to learn about your interviewing skills from fresh-in-your-mind experiences.

One particular criticism Stanley makes of Rick during the course of the interview is that he finds that Rick speaks "rather softly," wondering, "Can you be heard at the back of a classroom?" Rick responds by not only projecting but by projecting lines from a Shakespeare play he tells Stanley he performed in college ("and they could always hear me in the last row of the theater").

Feeling on a roll, Rick clinches the job (although he doesn't realize it at first) with a second gamble that also pays off. After hesitating, Rick decides to correct the English Department chair as to which of William Shakespeare's "Henry" plays contains the famous lines Rick recited (beginning with the line "Once more unto the breach, dear friends").

Stanley's "mistake" when he had conjectured the play to be *Henry the Fourth* was intentional; an English chair such as Stanley would most likely know that this famous quotation comes from *Henry the Fifth*; he is testing Rick's academic knowledge by asking Rick, "*Henry the Fourth*, wasn't it?" When Rick "politely" says, "I think it's *Henry the Fifth*," Stanley "nodded knowingly, more pleased now," and says, "Damn right it is." With his *very next words*, Stanley signals that the job is Rick's when he asks, "Can you be here Friday for an Organizational Meeting, Mr. Dadier?"

Were Rick and Stanley to be given a letter grade for their interviewing skills, Stanley would get an "A+" and Rick would get an "A." Wondering why Rick has

Are you in the right place? Knowing the kind of school you want –
and learning how to go about getting a position there

77

been denied the plus? What Rick does in the interview he does well, but he mostly neglects to use the interview to get additional insight into the school, its philosophy, its students, and its leadership. Had Rick succeeded more along these lines, he would have been in a better position to compare North Manual Trades with his "ideal" or "best-of-all-possible" school.

A commentary on accentuating special strengths during a job interview

One of the best things in general that Rick does in his job interview is that he comes up with specifics about his professional and personal experiences that keep Chair Stanley listening for more. Rick grounds his possession of the universally desired strong teacher voice in his non-professional acting experiences, but he clearly also demonstrates during the interview other important and usable connections between the professions of acting and teaching: presence, control, command, excitement, drama. These are all qualities that hold audiences – and classes – in rapt attention through a strong performance.

Rick also lets supervisor Stanley indirectly know that he recognizes and appreciates the importance of good supervision, telling Stanley he student taught at the vocational high school Machine and Metal Trades under Department Chairman Ackerman ("he helped me a lot, sir"); even better, Rick is smart enough and informed enough to realize that a school's reputation may not always be deserved ("it wasn't at all as bad as they'd painted it") – important to a boss whose all-boys' vocational school might be expected to have a less than wonderful reputation.

And, stereotypically, in an all-boys' school, it would certainly be considered a plus in a man-on-man interview that the job applicant comes across as "all man" – a Navy man, a war veteran, no less, as well as someone who was confident and comfortable in his masculine sense of self that he could go study to be a teacher at a college (New York City's Hunter College) still known by its only relatively recently shed (post World War II) all-female student body history. Rick repeatedly demonstrates an understanding of the importance of standing out from the other candidates for a job and selling yourself with energy in ways that are of significance to a particular school. Consider letting him be your mentor for your mock and real interviews.

Appointed teacher E. R. Braithwaite meets Headmaster Alex Florian of the Greenslade Secondary School

Like Rick Dadier, teacher E. R. Braithwaite also feels he's not financially in a position to turn down any job offer. (Both in the real world and the real world of novels, it's not often that we are.) But unlike Rick, Braithwaite, in the highly autobiographical novel *To Sir, With Love, is given* that option by Alex Florian, headmaster of a British secondary school. Braithwaite, in fact, goes on to consider saying "no, thank you" to an "official appointment" for a position the previous occupant abruptly resigned from.

Let's see what we can learn about knowing as much as possible about our "next" school from Braithwaite's experience that day, a day that begins with Mr. Florian's meeting briefly with Braithwaite and then telling him, as Braithwaite relates it to another teacher a little while later, to "take a look around to sort of see what's going on" before he decides whether to accept the appointment.

Braithwaite goes off on his own and on the basis of what he experiences that morning of the school's building and its students and teachers, he rather unenthusiastically decides to "have a shot" at the job: "I wanted this job badly and I was quite prepared to do it to the best of my ability, but it would be a job, not a labor of love." When you make this kind of distinction, you are far from having found your best-of-all-possible schools.

But when Braithwaite returns to the headmaster's office, where he had had *no interview* and, therefore, no opportunity to ask fact-finding or philosophy-finding questions, the headmaster, who had earlier only told Braithwaite that "things are done here somewhat differently from the usual run," proceeds to provide answers to such unasked questions as: "what is this school all about, anyway?" and "what are the students like?" and "how do you and your staff go about doing what you do here?" and "what is it you hope to accomplish?"

In fact, Mr. Florian's "interview with himself," as you will see, is more a mission statement on his school's "conceptual framework" than it is the kind of interview Chairman Stanley had with Rick Dadier in *The Blackboard Jungle.* Consider, then:

- *What are your thoughts and feelings about Mr. Florian's mission statement for Greenslade Secondary School?*
- *How close is it to the mission statement you would hope to hear from the principal of your ideal school?*
- *How enthusiastic would you be to "have a shot at the job" at Greenslade? Explain to Braithwaite why you think and feel the way you do.*

Mr. Florian tells Braithwaite, "You may have heard some talk about this school, Braithwaite. We're always being talked about, but unfortunately, most of the talk is by ill-informed people who are intolerant of the things we are trying to do here." To set the record straight for Braithwaite, Mr. Florian states up front that "the majority of the children here could be generally classified as difficult, probably because in Junior school they have shown some disregard for, or opposition to, authority."

Mr. Florian goes on to say, however, that "whether or not that authority was well-constituted is beside the point; it is enough to say that it depended largely on

Are you in the right place? Knowing the kind of school you want –
and learning how to go about getting a position there

79

fear, either of the stick or some other form of punishment. In the case of these children it failed. We in this school believe that children are merely men and women in process of development; and that that development, in all its aspects, should be neither forced nor restricted at the arbitrary whim of any individual who by some accident of fortune is in a position to exercise some authority over them."

Mr. Florian then dramatically specifies why punishment (or the threat of it) of these children for their "lack of interest" in school work is "unlikely" to bring out the best of them: "A child who has slept all night in a stuffy, overcrowded room, and then breakfasts on a cup of weak tea and a piece of bread, can hardly be expected to show a sharp, sustained interest in the abstractions of arithmetic, and the unrelated niceties of correct spelling."

As to the school behavior of such children, Mr. Florian sees it as "part of the general malaise which affects the whole neighborhood" that they live in and "produces a feeling of insecurity among the children." Instead of using coercion to discourage anti-social conduct, Greenslade Secondary School tries to give its students "affection, confidence, and guidance, more or less in that order, because experience has shown us that those are their most immediate needs."

Finally, Mr. Florian counters the talk of the ill-informed about Greenslade when he states that "it is said that here we practice free discipline. That's wrong, quite wrong. It would be more correct to say that we are seeking, as best we can, to establish disciplined freedom, that state in which the child feels free to work, play and express himself without fear of those whose job it is to direct and stimulate his efforts into constructive channels."

What will be Braithwaite's role be if he accepts the appointment to Greenslade? Mr. Florian makes it clear that "as teachers, we can help greatly if we become sufficiently important" to these children; "important enough for our influence to balance or even outweigh the evil . . . . Remember, they're wonderful children when you get to know them, and somehow, I think you will. Good luck."

A commentary on your mission to discover a school's mission

Whether your professional goal is to find "a job" or "*the* job," the process of job-hunting should include learning as much as you can about a particular school, department, student body, faculty, or educational leader. This last is really important; the principal of a school sets the tone of and for the school. In effect, you need to know exactly *why* you would accept or decline a position should you be offered one. A caution: do not count on being presented with the kind of informative disquisition provided E. R. Braithwaite by Headmaster Florian. (Had Braithwaite heard the headmaster's "statement" before he took a look around the school, he would have undoubtedly been much more enthusiastic about having "a shot" at the job.)

Even when you have done your before-the-interview homework and believe that this is *not* somewhere *you* want to work or someone *you* want to work for, go to that interview, anyway: the experience and your later analysis of it is good practice for your next interview. Also, your realization and your reasons that you do not want to work at a particular school may actually come to you during the interview itself.

Most interviews provide some direct and indirect opportunities to verify and clarify what you have already researched about a school. Because the more you know in advance the better, you should network with *anyone* who might have "the word on the street" about a school you're interested in, as well as research the official word. Locate and "study" governmental and school publications like annually produced school "report cards" and frequently revised and always fact-filled school directories. You will also want to do Internet searches for newspaper and magazine articles on a school and its students and faculty and on the community it serves; you may also be able to make contact with current and former staff and students, this year's student teachers, and recent alumni.

Realistically, you can't possibly during an interview pursue all the questions you have researched and thought about in advance, and you will probably have to settle for partial answers to those you get to ask. Nevertheless, you should be prepared with those questions that are most important to you so that you can try to weave them into the fabric of the interview. Be alert for opportunities from interviewers and work at creating your own. You should have more than a "gut feeling" about the answers you hope to hear.

In addition, your coming across as being this well prepared, as well caring enough to want to know, can be the "deal maker" because your pursuit of these kinds of questions during the interview can show your potential employer that you have a comprehensive understanding of what "life" in a school can be like, may be like, should be like.

Meet Tom Mason and a faculty that is "schooled in murder"

"Life" is literally "murder" in the Chicago area high school at the center of Mark Richard Zubro's 2008 mystery novel *Schooled in Murder*: a faculty member is found dead in a supply room after she stormed out of a particularly rancorous English department meeting (these things happen – not murder, usually, but rancorous department meetings). Fellow teachers, not students, are the prime suspects.

As you "attend" this meeting, which opens the novel, you'll find that you can't help but think about many of the ways this school's usual and daily mode of operation could be "fatal" to your interest in teaching as a career choice. However, if you think beyond those initial depressing thoughts, you might discover that you

Are you in the right place? Knowing the kind of school you want –
and learning how to go about getting a position there

81

are in a position *right now* to make certain specific recommendations that could bring this faculty together. Feel free starting now.

Chapter 1 begins: "The screaming didn't start until fifteen minutes after the torment stopped. It was a typical faculty meeting, or at least, typical for this faculty. Bored to tears or furiously battling, the assembled members of the Grover Cleveland High School English department rivaled, in irrationality and intractability, the disputes among the most virulent warring religious factions on the planet."

In its second paragraph, Chapter 1 introduces Mabel Spandrel, head of English – and what the reader hears about her from the teacher-narrator's perspective is in sharp contrast to what can be inferred about English Chairman Stanley of *The Blackboard Jungle*. Specifying what the "torture" in the opening sentence of the novel referred to, the narrator states that "the initial torture consisted of the mind-numbingly boring speech delivered at the onset of every meeting by Mabel Spandrel," adding that "she had a soft voice that droned from opening syllable to closing pluperfect subjunctive verb . . . . I could picture the punctuation in her speeches pleading for release."

If you are also beginning to have a first impression of the novel's teacher-narrator (Tom Mason by name), Tom quickly adds that "I, however, was not about to join the cynics in the back who placed bets on and then counted how many times she used the phrase 'educational leaders.'"

Tom Mason continues his portrait of Mabel Spandrel (one that may resonate for those of you who have encountered the most negative extreme of educational "leadership"): "Behind Mabel's boring exterior lured the heart of a python combined with the cunning of a particularly petrified rock. She was dangerous enough as a dolt. Give her a dose of intelligence and there was no telling what ghastly calamities she might perpetrate."

Concluding his portrait, Tom zeroes in on a major and very current criticism of contemporary educational leadership: "She had a business background and had never spent a minute in a classroom, until she got here, a surefire guarantee of an attitude of contempt from veteran teachers. Getting business people into schools had been a big trend for several years. And if kids were widgets, it might have made sense."

With "veteran teachers" making up one of the major factions a conventional secondary school can be split into, the other major faction is often much newer and younger teachers and their "wild ambition." However, Tom will soon add that he "loved the passion of these new college graduates and their allies" but "hated their blind adherence to the latest education trends."

In the fictional but of course very believable life of Grover Cleveland High School in *Schooled for Murder*, these two political factions are further split *by tactics* into "the suckups" and "the non-suckups." (Tom tells us up front: "I hate suck-ups.") Noting that many of the non-suckups were the old guard, Tom complains that too many of them adhered fervently to the dictum "I've done it this way since dirt, and you can't make me change."

Tom believes that "a whole bunch of folks in this faction needed swift kicks in the butt." Despite his sympathies with the old guard, Tom is "sick to death" of them because although he "understood, all too well" the arguments for their position, a lot of the old guard were "close-minded dinosaurs who refused to admit that maybe what they were doing in their classrooms wasn't the most effective approach."

Of course, Tom concludes:

> Once in a while a brave soul would dare to suggest that both sides of the new-versus-old techniques factions were talking about the same thing except that now some boob in college academia had given a random educational process or approach a new name. This, of course, was heresy. Far more important to impose your trendy or traditional education philosophy or psychology or methodology or vocabulary on the unwilling . . . . Petty debates about silly privileges among those who educate the children of this world? You better believe it.

A commentary on schools that can be "murder"

All too often and all too frustratingly, a school can be metaphorical "murder" – and there's really no mystery as to why. It's interesting that the word "faculty" in its Latin origins means "power" since political power in any school is exactly what a split-down-the-middle group of teachers is often fighting for. Beware being a pawn in the games faculty factions "power play" or you'll get caught between the so-called "visionary" rebel group that is out and trying to get in and the so-called "upholding standards" old guard that is in and trying to remain so. Labels like "tried and true" and "researched-based" will be tossed about, minds will close down while mouths open wide, and true teaching and real learning will suffer as collateral damage in an ongoing war.

Two things to keep in mind amidst the clamor:

- Last time anyone looked, the wheel as it was invented was still working the way it was meant to. If it's not working that way in your school, as good teachers, supervisors and administrators, you should take a look and learn how the wheel is spinning in other schools.
- Just because a teacher has been teaching the same way for the past (fill in the blank: days, months, years) doesn't mean that that way was all that good even on Day One.

Are you in the right place? Knowing the kind of school you want –
and learning how to go about getting a position there

83

Tom Mason in *Schooled in Murder* tries to stay above the fray at Grover Cleveland High School – a position tantamount to levitation. (It doesn't help – though it makes the story – that Tom Mason is the school's union representative as well as an amateur detective with a record of solving crimes.)

But as a new teacher you would not *choose* to be in his shoes or his school. So here is an assortment of questions culled from the experiences of students, student teachers, teachers, supervisors, and administrators to help you prepare to find the right school for you. You can't possibly get all of the following questions answered during the course of your research into a school; however, why not keep them for future reference: you will find them helpful in learning about your school and your place in it – once you start to become part of that school's ongoing history.

A commentary – in the form of questions – so that you will not wind up being a fatalist about your first school

- What is the school's philosophy of teaching and learning and how does it compare with your own? Is the school's philosophy clearly reflected in its mission statement and in any annual evaluation rating or school report card?
- How diverse is the student body and teaching staff?
- What specifics about the school's curriculum and courses of study excite or trouble you? What relationships and programs exist among various departments and disciplines?
- Do teachers' administrative duties seem to have priority over teaching and learning?
- What policies regarding class work, homework, assessment, and discipline are in place and in practice?
- What variety of student assessment is used and how much of the teaching in place smacks of "teaching to the test"?
- What texts are in use and how often are they re-evaluated and replaced?
- Which remedial and accelerated programs exist for students with special needs?
- What do the co-curricular and extra-curricular programs consist of and how many students take part in them?
- What support, guidance, and counseling services (medical, emotional, psychological) does the school provide to students and to their parents?
- How up-to-date and well-maintained is the school's physical plant?
- How strong is the parents' association, and what community-building programs exist?
- How strong is the alumni association, and does it show its strength by reinvesting in the school?

- With respect to new teachers, is the school atmosphere collegial? Supportive? Overly judgmental? Is criticism constructive? Is there institutionalized mentoring?

- Are administrators' doors open and are key personnel more than movers of paper? Are they receptive listeners, or do they start with "no" and make you work long and hard at convincing them?

- Are the principal and her or his supervisory staff "there" for teachers and students or is leadership top down, "by appointment only"?

- How long have the principal and other key supervisory leaders been with the school? Is the person who put his or her stamp on the school or department scheduled for leave of absence, transfer, or retirement?

- What does leadership look for in lesson planning, structuring, and execution?

- Do teachers work together on curriculum revision, inter-disciplinary studies, co-planning, co-teaching? Are there factions pitting newcomers against veterans?

- What awards and honors have been bestowed on the school, its recent students, and current faculty?

- What are the school, the department, the student body, and the faculty known for in the community?

Other questions will definitely occur to you from your experiences as a student teacher, as a participant in a secondary school's field observation program, as a substitute or part-time teacher, and from the workload of your academic and education courses (readings, assignments, projects, activities and class discussions).

Also, since memories are made of this, it's worth your while to think back on those "good old" and perhaps "not-so-good-old" days when you were a high school student: what specifically was there about the school you graduated from that would make you want to return there to teach? What was there that would make you say "no, never"?

A commentary on "no, never; not that school!"

In Dan Elish's 2008 novel *The Misadventures of Justin Hearnfeld*, the title character vows on the day of his high school graduation that "he would never set foot in the building again. High School was over. Life simply had to get better."

Four years later, Justin Hearnfeld, having just completed college, makes the "fateful decision" to return to that very same high school – "the scene of four years of misery" – as a new teacher in its English Department.

Thinking back on your own high school days as a way of thinking ahead to the kind of school you would want to teach in is no academic exercise.

Are you in the right place? Knowing the kind of school you want –
and learning how to go about getting a position there

85

Experience-based comparisons between the secondary school you probably know best – it's your alma mater, after all – and others you would consider working in are not that difficult to make and can be distinctly productive.

As with all such comparisons and contrasts (for example, with the school you student taught in), your focus should be on discovering as much as you can about why you want to (or don't want to) work in a particular school with a particular program under a particular leadership. If your ideal school is the "best of all possible schools," that doesn't mean you can't find it with the "map" this chapter provides: after all, it's the best of all *possible* schools.

As English Department Chair Stanley put it to Rick Dadier in *The Blackboard Jungle,* "Why do you want to teach here?"

Glad you asked.

6

Your "way to be" and your "way to go": your teacher persona as a reflection of your educational philosophy

*T*he saddest chapter in this book presents "case studies" from two British novels on *how misconceived philosophies of education can lead to personal and professional tragedy for students and teachers alike*

Cast of Characters

Thomas Gradgrind, *the veteran educational theorist and school "superintendent" from* Hard Times *by Charles Dickens, Great Britain, 19th-century classic (1854)*

Ursula Brangwen, *the brand-new and very young neighborhood school teacher from* The Rainbow *by D. H. Lawrence, Great Britain, 20*[h]*-century classic (1915) (fictional teacher #21)*

Introduction to the case study of Thomas Gradgrind (and company!): the fanatical "educationist" pays a visit to one of his "model" classrooms

What kind of education theorist and teacher supervisor would the classic British author Charles Dickens produce if that nineteenth-century master of satiric grotesquerie were to create the embodiment of *misguided* educational philosophy?

Well, as we know from Chapter 3 of *So You Think You Might Like to Teach,* Dickens would create Thomas Gradgrind, whose "model" school is held up for ridicule and scorn in the opening pages of the novel *Hard Times.*

Thomas Gradgrind is "a man of realities," "a man of facts and calculations." As an educator who "proceeds upon the principle that two and two are four, and nothing over, and who is not to be talked into allowing for anything over," Thomas Gradgrind practices what he preaches. And, as a supervisor of teachers, Mr. Gradgrind oversees to make certain that everyone in his model school is in complete lockstep with his educational philosophy.

Make no mistake about it, as a new teacher you will see in every aspect of your teaching the practical effects of your foundational philosophy. Your "way to go" (your teaching philosophy) informs and helps create your "way to be" (your teaching persona); it is the vision behind what your teaching looks like in operation. Reflect on your philosophy and you'll see your persona in the mirror.

Teachers may not always outwardly preach what they believe, but what they believe underlies what they practice. Thomas Gradgrind believes, preaches, and practices – and the consequences of Mr. Gradgrind's misconceived vision are dire. As Dickens tells us, the result is the "murdering" of innocent young children by the *systematic* destruction of their "imaginations" and their sense of "wonder." The ultimate effect of Mr. Gradgrind's educational theory is to produce a classroom that contains a large number of pupils who, in practice, are "brain dead."

As Dickens summarizes it, Mr. Gradgrind fanatically believes that "the one thing needful" is that "gallons of facts" – and nothing else – be "poured" into boys and girls by their teachers. Today, this is sometimes known as "the banking model" of teaching because "deposits" are repeatedly being made (through excessive lecturing and through "teaching to the test"). A third familiar comparison is the metaphor of the student as "a clean slate" to be written on by the "wisdom" of the teacher.

On a "fact-finding" visit to the "plain, bare, monotonous vault of a school-room" of his model primary school, Mr. Gradgrind emphatically intones his supervisory "observations" to two other individuals: the local schoolmaster and an unidentified "gentleman" visitor. Mr. Gradgrind's observations are haughty and "horticultural": "teach these boys and girls nothing but Facts," Mr. Gradgrind commands. "Facts alone," he continues, "are wanted in life. Plant nothing else, and root out everything else. You can only form the minds of reasoning animals upon Facts: nothing else will ever be of any service to them."

A commentary on how a misconceived educational philosophy makes educational practice imperfect

Early in *Hard Times*, in the course of his supervisory visit, Mr. Gradgrind calls on a young girl to "define a horse." However, the child is so "thrown into the greatest alarm by this demand" that she is rendered speechless. Has this ever happened to you as a student? Have you ever unintentionally caused this extreme reaction in a student of yours?

Misinterpreting the girl's silence, an astonished Mr. Gradgrind declares the pupil to be "possessed of no facts, in reference to one of the commonest of animals!" However, just because there is nothing coming out of this young girl's mouth does not automatically mean that there is nothing going on in her head.

Because Thomas Gradgrind is interested *only* in regurgitated "right" answers from rote-memorized facts, he has zero tolerance for "ignorance" and absolutely no interest in a teacher's using a wrong answer as the starting point for stimulating thinking and building learning. Today's "descendants" of Mr. Gradgrind fall into the insecure teacher trap of assuming that student silence after a teacher's question means absence of knowledge, or lack of interest, or reluctance to reason, or inability to think. They truly do not know what to make of it.

Jumping to one or more of these wrong conclusions (which hardly models critical thinking skills!), these teachers immediately get nervous ("I'll never complete my lesson plan for today!"). Their "solution" to this timing and pacing problem is often to answer their own question or call on the "fastest hand in the class," as though it were a life preserver from the Titanic.

Eternally grateful to those few students who raise their hands after almost every question (no silence now), these teachers fall into the pattern of teaching every day to only a small core group; the rest of the class becomes "audience" (which, although the word literally means "a group of listeners," does not guarantee that active listening is actually occurring). In addition, students whose hands don't fly up *because* they are working at reflecting wind up having their thinking cut short.

What these fearful teachers have actually taught the bulk of their students is how to play and win the game "Wait 'Em Out." As its name suggests, when a core of classmates can always be counted on to come to the teacher's rescue, the rest of the students just have to wait until a handful of hands goes up and they will be excused from the hard work of thinking and participating.

Some of these worried teachers who mistakenly think that good teaching always reveals itself in an immediate show of hands do, *at times*, feel guilty about the sparse "showing." Because these times can be during supervisory visits, supervisors have gotten wise to a certain ruse: guilty-feeling teachers tell their students that for some of the questions asked, they should raise their right hand if they know the answer and their left if they don't. Only the "righties" will get called on.

Good teachers realize that their job is made up of two creative acts: planning lessons with care and executing them with style. Valuing critical and creative thinking in their classrooms, these teachers spend a great deal of their non-teaching time preparing their objectives, their materials, their motivating activities, and their lessons filled with well-worded thought-provoking questions.

Teachers across the curriculum who understand the craft (and art) of questioning ask an assortment of different types of questions, including fact questions and questions that require and stimulate thinking about an established set of facts. These teachers understand, respect, and honor "the sound of silence," the time needed by most students to think first about the meaning of a teacher's substantive question and then work on formulating a response.

Because these teachers do not go into "pedagogical panic" during the first moments of silence after a question, they also do not succumb to the temptation to either answer their own question or unnecessarily repeat or rephrase it. Instead, they recognize that although different students may require different amounts of "processing" time, all students deserve the opportunity to mull, ponder, reflect, and speculate. In truth, good teachers expect and require something like the following to be going on in their students' heads when they're asked thought-provoking questions of consequence:

> *Hmm, what is it that question is actually asking? Well, that's pretty provocative. I'm interested. You've got me (I don't mean I'm stumped; I mean I'm hooked, intrigued). But do I have any thoughts on this? Well, let me think about what they might be.*

In Dickens's narrative in *Hard Times*, when Mr. Gradgrind does not get the instantaneous answer he has demanded from the young girl he called on for "the definition of a horse," he immediately requests it from a second non-volunteer. That young boy, physically manifesting the "squeeze" that has been put on him, raises "his knuckles to his freckled forehead."

He then recites (without stopping for air!) what he has been repeatedly spoon-fed and has dutifully committed to memory: "Quadruped. Graminivorous. Forty teeth, namely, twenty-four grinders, four eye-teeth, and twelve incisive. Sheds coat in the spring; in marshy countries, sheds hoofs, too. Hoofs hard, but requiring to be shod with iron. Age known by marks in mouth."

And before you come up for air: what is your *gut reaction* to this pupil's answer – and what do you think Mr. Gradgrind's *professional reaction* might be? Thoughts as to why?

And, oh yes, how would you expect *a student of yours* to define a horse – or, if you prefer, how would *you* define a horse?

A commentary on the meanings we make as we make sense of our world

Extremely gratified by the answer he gets from the young boy, Mr. Gradgrind turns to the young girl and declares: "Now . . . you know what a horse is." Mr. Gradgrind's educational philosophy is grounded in the dual belief that the teacher is the sole source of wisdom in the classroom (the teacher as "the font" of knowledge) and that young people, *by their very nature*, would never embrace, let alone seek out, knowledge that has not been crammed into them.

Regrettably, this philosophy is still "alive and ill" in some contemporary classrooms. Have you ever encountered examples (it is hoped, somewhat less grotesque) of this "cram-it-into-their-heads-against-their-will" conception of education? How Dickensian was it?

In connection with this critical question of how knowledge is "imparted" and understanding achieved, it is important for you to ask yourself as a new or prospective teacher (of English, or social studies, or math, or the sciences, or the arts) what the role of "definitions" is in your particular subject area. Do you see their role any differently now – that is, after the experience you have just had with the *definition* of a horse? Why or why not?

Which of the most frequently used "definitions of terms" in your subject area read like representations of reality, representations of the real world? Which read more like the kind of old-fashioned, abstract dictionary definition represented by the Dickensian definition of "a horse"? In other words, how many of your subject area's definitions make "descriptive" sense (telling it like it is)? How many come across sounding "prescriptive" (telling it like some one says it should be)?

A student's critical thinking about a subject area (social studies, literature, biology, language, physics, mathematics, art, chemistry, music, you name it) can only be done using the actual *content* of that subject area. When human beings think, they think about "something" – some "thing." Good teachers always assess that their students know the facts that they need to make use of when called upon to engage in even the lowest level of the thinking process. No one can be thinking about "nothing" – although that is sometimes what young people say they are thinking about when directly asked by an adult, "What are you thinking?" (More often than not, the adult is the parent.)

Whatever your subject area, it is essential that the key terms in your field get defined in ways that are as concrete, specific, functional, operational, and visual as possible. Critical thinking across the subject areas starts with particular observations, makes connections among these specific details, discovers patterns across the connections, and draws tentative conclusions from them.

No teacher of any subject can effectively teach that subject without simultaneously teaching students how to think critically within the subject's specific content. Evidence, data, facts – these raw materials are necessary for true thinking and real understanding. Raw materials are always descriptive, never prescriptive. So the more descriptive the definitions of a field of study's key terms, the more likely it is that students will remember and comprehend the significance of the raw material they are being asked to analyze, synthesize, and draw inferences from.

Introduction to the case study of Ursula Brangwen (and company!): a graduating secondary school student becomes the regular teacher of students just a few years younger than herself – but see what happens to a dream destroyed

If Thomas Gradgrind is the "murderer" of the essence of childhood – its sense of wonder and of the imagination, then the veteran teachers who advise Ursula Brangwen, a young girl and brand-new teacher in D. H. Lawrence's novel *The*

Rainbow (the prequel to Lawrence's novel *Women in Love*), are the "murderers" of
Ursula's idealism, her sense of self-worth, her professional identity, and, ultimately,
her pedagogical soul.

The Rainbow, like *Hard Times*, is set in small town England in the nineteenth
century. And also like the Dickens novel (but with stark realism in place of the
satire), *The Rainbow* is universal and timeless in what it can teach about teachers
and students and about schools and classrooms both ideal and less than.

Just seventeen years old, Miss Ursula Brangwen has begun her teaching career
working with students who are not that much younger than she is – and she is
floundering. Some of you as student teachers may be only a few years older than
Ursula and, like her, are hungry for help. Also like Ursula, you may have gravitated
toward that place where teacher advice flows freely, whether solicited or not: a
school's teacher room or faculty lounge. Ursula finds two veteran teachers, Miss
Harby and Mr. Brunt, present. And, in the course of "teacher talk," she confesses
to a feeling of being "frightened" in her classroom.

You may not have yet set foot in an actual teachers' room (proceed
cautiously when you do!), but, for now, make the most of your imagination and
put yourself into Ursula's shoes as she listens to the snippets of philosophy and
advice that Miss Harby and Mr. Brunt are only too happy to offer. How do you
think Ursula feels – how do *you* feel – about what these veteran teachers have
passed on and the manner in which their words of wisdom have been passed
down?

As she enters the teachers' room, Miss Harby overhears Ursula trying to
explain to those present (including Mr. Brunt) why she feels "frightened."
Hesitatingly, Ursula begins, "The children seem so . . . ," only to be interrupted by
Mss Harby's "What?" Ursula replies with an uneasy laugh, "Why, Mr. Brunt says I
ought to tackle my class."

Miss Harby responds to hearing this in a manner that Lawrence tells the
reader is "hard, superior, and trite": "Oh, you have to keep order if you want to
teach." Ursula doesn't comment and Lawrence lets the reader know that she "feels
"non valid before them."

It is Mr. Brunt's cue to jump in: "If you want to be let to *live*," he stresses, "you
have." After Miss Harby interjects her "Well, if you can't keep order, what good are
you?," Mr. Brunt adds his clincher that if Ursula truly wants to at least survive in
her classroom (through the imposition of classroom order), then, "you've got to
do it by yourself." His voice rising like the "bitter cry of the prophets," Mr. Brunt
concludes: "You'll get no help from anybody."

In a kind of "amen" to that, Miss Harby concurs: "Oh, indeed!," adding as her
final word on the subject, "Some people can't be helped."

A commentary on battle cries from the faculty lounge

Strictly speaking, "strict" is exactly how Mr. Brunt and Miss Harby (who happens to be the headmaster's wife) come across. With her "hard, superior, trite" emphasis on "order," the veteran Miss Harby will sound her battle cry and have her say (like a font of "wisdom" or like Mr. Brunt's "cry of the prophets"): "If you can't keep order, what good are you?"

With that, Miss Harby's "collegial" work is done. She exits the faculty lounge, her teacher persona (her "way to be") and its complementary educational philosophy (her "way to go") unruffled, unmoved, and completely intact. Mind her – or suffer the consequences. (You met some of Miss Harby's counterparts from a full century later in Chapter 2's examination of teacher persona. The more things change, the more they remain the same?)

Perhaps Miss Harby and Mr. Brunt made you think of drill sergeants mapping battles in some unending war between teachers and students: a life or death struggle ("if you want to be let to live"), in which only labels like "enemy" and "victor" and "vanquished" appear applicable.

Or perhaps you saw a "power play" or sports event ("Mr. Brunt says I ought to tackle my class"). Still, none of these comparisons is comforting: it's a competitive, not a co-operative, world out there in these veterans' classrooms, a place where the concept of a "community of learners" is both foreign and strange.

Have you encountered your own share of "Mr. Brunts" and "Miss Harbys"? Would you choose them as role models? Should a mentor (your on-site co-operating teacher, your college program's field supervisor, your colleagues, your chairperson, your grade leader, your principal) make a new teacher feel "non-valid" and unworthy of or beyond help, as these veterans make Ursula feel?

Those of us in the field of education who have mentored in 21st-century schools would bristle at Mr. Brunt's remark that ". . . you've got to do it by yourself . . . . You'll get no help from anybody." But is there a grain of truth to Mr. Brunt's self-satisfied declaration? Will you as a new teacher have to *hope* that you will be in the kind of school where the supervisory leadership is truly supportive and not prone to snap judgments and harsh putdowns like Miss Harby's "some people can't be helped"?

Ursula Brangwen now finds herself in "a very deep mess"

A little bit on, the author D. H. Lawrence tells us that Ursula feels herself to be "in a very deep mess" soon after her visit to the faculty lounge. Ursula worries that unless she quickly "finds herself" in her classroom, finds *her* true teacher persona and its complementary philosophy of education, she will be lost to teaching forever. Seventeen-year-old Ursula Brangwen is tormented by the thought that because she has not *won over* her students, her only recourse is to consider them the "enemy" in a war *she* must win. Will she have to become like an automaton, an unfeeling machine, in order to control her students and "manage" her classroom?

Left now to her own devices by her "colleagues" and feeling pressed to quickly "find herself" if she is to survive as a teacher, an insecure Ursula undergoes in her thinking and behavior in the pages that follow the scene in the teachers' room a "transformation" from actively teaching the students who make up her class to "managing" her classroom; it is a transformation that the reader may not be surprised by but will be shocked by.

To truly appreciate Ursula's transformation, it is critical to keep in mind that the *foundation* belief among the Harbys and Brunts of Ursula's educational world and, therefore, the oppressive belief that Ursula has been struggling with as she works on her "way to be" in the classroom is that "children will never naturally acquiesce to sitting in a class and submitting to knowledge. They must be compelled by a stronger, wiser will. Against which will they must always strive to revolt."

Therefore, it follows philosophically and practically that "the first great effort of every teacher of a large class must be to bring the will of the children into accordance with his own will. And this he can only do by an abnegation of his personal self, and an application of a system of laws . . . ."

In contrast, and like so many starting-out teachers to this day, Ursula was initially convinced that she was going to prove to be "the first wise teacher." How? Simple: subvert the foundation belief of the Harbys and Brunts "by making the whole business personal, and using no compulsion." Ursula "believed entirely in her own personality." Sound familiar?

A commentary on Ursula's less than ideal school

No wonder Ursula feels she is "in a very deep mess." Not only has she placed herself and her philosophy in opposition to that of the headmaster of her school but she has, in effect, taken him on personally and given ammunition to his supporters on the faculty. In addition, she has made the naive assumption that her loss of the support of her boss and her colleagues will be more than made up for by the support she will gain from her students. However, as Lawrence points out, "she was offering to a class a relationship which only one or two of the children were sensitive enough to appreciate, so the mass were left outsiders, therefore against her."

"The invincible iron" closes on Ursula as she sets as her teaching purpose "making them know so much each day"

At the beginning of her transformation, Ursula wonders about the educational life of her school: "It was horrible – all hate! Must she be like this? She could feel the ghastly necessity. She must become the same – put away the personal self, become an instrument, an abstraction, working upon a certain material, the class, to achieve a set purpose of making them know so much each day. And she could not submit. Yet gradually she felt the invincible iron closing upon her."

And by the end of her transformation, Ursula, at last "distant and impersonal," was like the other teachers: "she saw no longer the child, how his eyes danced, or how he had a queer little soul that could not be bothered with shaping hand-writing so long as he dashed down what he thought. She saw no children, only the task that was to be done. And keeping her eyes there, on the task, and not on the child, she was impersonal enough to punish where she could otherwise only have sympathized, understood, and condoned . . . ."

A commentary on "classroom management" and teaching a class

It might be instructive, at this point, to recall the word "discipline." If the first thought that comes into your mind when you hear the "D" word is "order" (as in Miss Harby's mantra that "if you can't keep order, what good are you?"), then you need to be careful that "discipline" in your classroom doesn't become "regimentation" for your students – along with "punishment for breaking the established rules."

Somehow, in regimented classrooms, approbation, positive reinforcement, and other kinds of rewards for students who follow meaningful (and carefully explained and reviewed) procedures are, sadly, often absent or given only lip service. However, punishments follow fast upon infractions, violations, "crimes," and "breakings of commandments." Since the word "discipline" comes from "disciple," it would seem that, literally and actually, the better "way to go" would be to create through good *teaching* practices a class of "disciples" – students who have been *motivated to discipline themselves* to the rigors of learning.

In her idealism and naivete, Ursula Brangwen somewhat presumptuously sees herself, D. H. Lawrence tells us, as "the first wise teacher." This may not be the best starting off point to grow and develop from; nevertheless, it is not an uncommon attitude among some novice teachers even today. This understandable (and forgivable) trait of the brand-new teacher is "child's play," however, compared with the destructive philosophy of education of Ursula's experienced colleagues.

For the Harbys and Brunts of the world, the process of education must, philosophically, be seen as a battle of wills: students versus teachers, teachers versus students. Children, the argument goes, will always "strive to revolt" against knowledge; they will never acquiesce to sitting in a class and submitting to knowledge." It follows, then, that in this "natural" war, all "calls to battle" must be immediately answered. And since adults know best, knowledge, like spinach, becomes what adults need to force down children's immature throats (minds) because, though it may not be to their taste, it is for their own good.

The educational philosophy that Lawrence himself would more likely subscribe to is closer to what the term "to educate" means in its original Latin: "to lead out." Good teaching involves not a "shoving into" the student's mind all of the teacher's knowledge, understanding, and accumulated wisdom but a planned program, within a conducive setting, of methodologies, materials, questions, activities, and practices that enables teachers to "lead out" the thinking that they have stimulated in their students' minds.

Faced with daily disorder and possible future chaos in her classroom, the well-meaning but fearful and unconfident 17-year-old Ursula Brangwen comes to think that she needs to abandon her belief in her own personhood (an "abnegation" of self); she must become the abstract representation of the "laws" of adolescent nature and psychology, as they have been divined by and enshrined in those teachers like Mr. Brunt and Miss Harby who are far more experienced than she is.

Because Ursula is very young and ungrounded in a much needed, well thoughtout educational philosophy of her own, she has more of a dream of her ideal classroom than a vision for its enactment. Feeling the pressure of "the system," Ursula decides she *must* resolve to become "an instrument, an abstraction, working upon a certain material, the class, to achieve a set purpose of making them know so much each day." Ursula strives to turn herself into a machine-like taskmaster. The "invincible iron" closes upon her will and makes Ursula into some "thing," an unfeeling, inhumane, ultimately inhuman abstraction of "will power" in total control of the enemy called her "students."

Does Ursula's classroom sound like the kind of place you would like to be a student in? A teacher in? (Been there? Care to elaborate?)

Does Ursula's school remind you of other kinds of "institutions"? Do prisons, insane asylums, factories, hospitals come to mind? Any others? What is it about the way of life – the "way to be," the "way to go" – in these institutions?

As Ursula proceeds to put into practice her newly adopted philosophy of education, an "incident" occurs between Ursula and one of her more difficult students, Williams. However, the incident is anything but incidental; it is actually the playing out (see Chapter 3 of this book) of one of the most classic games of Teacher vs. Student and Student vs. Teacher.

By the way, a secondary failing an inexperienced teacher like Ursula demonstrates during the upcoming scene is that she assigns and frames as punishment certain academic activities across the curriculum that subject teachers all need, on the contrary, to motivate their students to see the value of. Take note of where Ursula does this to the activity of writing (both in school and at home), the whole concept of homework, and the pedagogical practice of assigning silent reading on school time. Can you spot, too, where Ursula commits the cardinal teaching error of making a threat to a student that she cannot or knows she will not follow through on? Uh-oh!

As you experience the scene between Teacher Ursula and Student Williams, many of the following questions will arise naturally without the scene's losing its grip on you;

An incident that proves hardly incidental between student and teacher in the 1915 novel *The Rainbow* by D. H. Lawrence

This scene from more than a century ago opens with Ursula's determining that "she would assert himself for mastery, be only teacher. She was set now. She was going to fight and subdue" since she now knew who her "enemies" were in the class. The one she hated the most was Williams:

> He was a sort of defective, not bad enough to be so classified. He could read with fluency, and had plenty of cunning intelligence. But he could not keep still. And he had a kind of sickness very repulsive to a sensitive girl, something cunning and etiolated and degenerate. Once he had thrown an ink-well at her, in one of his mad little rages. Twice he had run home out of class. He was a well-known character.

Williams, employing his "cunning intelligence," would sometimes hang around Ursula and fawn on her, but this, not surprisingly, would make Ursula dislike him even more. From one of the other students in the class Ursula had previously taken "a supple cane, and this she determined to use when real occasion came." The occasion presents itself, one morning, as the class is engaged in an extended writing activity; moving around the room (teachers circulate during such times to this day), Ursula notices a fairly large dark smudge on Williams's composition paper, and a verbal Teacher vs. Student game commences as soon as Ursula begins to question Williams with: "Why have you made this blot?" Williams responds by countering:

"Please, miss, it fell off my pen," he whined out, in the mocking voice
that he was so clever in using. The boys near snorted with laughter. For
Williams was an actor, he could tickle the feelings of his hearers subtly.
Particularly he could tickle the children with him into ridiculing his
teacher, or indeed, any authority of which he was not afraid.

Ursula's next move in the game – which goes "against her usual sense of
justice, and the boy resented it derisively" – is to say: "Then you must stay in and
finish another page of composition." However, after some time has gone by and it
is now twelve noon, Ursula catches Williams as he tries to slink out and tells him to
sit back down: "And there she sat, and there he sat, alone, opposite to her, on the
back desk, looking up at her with his furtive eyes every minute."

Some more time goes by and then Williams "insolently" calls out to Ursula,
"Please, miss, I've got to go an errand." Ursula tells him to bring his composition
book up to her so she can see how much he has written; he does, making certain
to noisily flap his book along the desks. When she examines his book, Ursula sees
that Williams has not written a single line:

"Go back and do the writing you have to do," said Ursula. And she sat at
her desk, trying to correct books. She was trembling and upset. And for
an hour the miserable boy writhed and grinned in his seat. At the end of
that time he had done five lines.

"As it is so late now," Ursula then tells Williams, "you will finish the rest this
evening." The boy kicks his way insolently out of the classroom. Later in the
afternoon when the students have all returned from their recess and are seated,
Ursula and Williams, we are told by Lawrence, are still eyeing each other, and
Ursula's heart beats "thick" because she "knew it was a fight between them."

During a session on geography, as a way to attract the attention of other boys
and disrupt Ursula's lesson, Williams can be seen continually ducking his head
under his desk. Ursula twice interrupts her lesson to ask Williams the identical
question – "What are you doing?" Williams, now so well into the game that Teacher
and Student are playing, "lifted his face, the sore-rimmed eyes half smiling," and
grudgingly responds: "Nothing," managing to come across, Lawrence tells us, as
both "triumphant" and "aggrieved."

Because Ursula, according to Lawrence, finds "something intrinsically
indecent" about Williams, she shrinks away from the boy who, Lawrence adds, was
a match even for Mr. Harby: "He was so persistent, so cringing, and flexible, he
howled so when he was hurt, that the master hated more the teacher who sent him
than he hated the boy himself. For of the boy he was sick of the sight."

Resuming the geography lesson, Ursula is aware of "a little ferment in the class. Williams' spirit infected them all." Ursula hears a scuffle, and fearing that she will be "beaten" if the other students now turn on her, she orders Williams to the front of the room after Williams makes faces at another student and "nips" the leg of a second. But Williams refuses to obey: "I shan't," he snarls, rat-like, grinning. And then something "went click in Ursula's soul":

> Her face and eyes set, she went through the class straight. The boy cowered before her glowering, fixed eyes. But she advanced on him, seized him by the arm, and dragged him from his seat. He clung to the form. It was the battle between him and her. Her instinct had suddenly become calm and quick. She jerked him from his grip, and dragged him, struggling and kicking, to the front. He kicked her several times, and clung to the forms as he passed, but she went on. The class was on its feet in excitement. She saw it, and made no move.

Because Williams has a history of running out of her class, Ursula knows that if she lets go of the boy he will dash to the door. Instead, she snatches her "supple" cane from the desk, and brings it down on him:

> She saw his face beneath her, white, with eyes like the eyes of a fish, stony, yet full of hate and horrible fear. And she loathed him, the hideous writhing thing that was nearly too much for her. In horror lest he should overcome her, and yet at the heart quite calm, she brought down the cane again and again, whilst he struggled making inarticulate noises, and lunging vicious kicks at her. With one hand she managed to hold him, and now and then the cane came down on him. He writhed, like a mad thing. But the pain of the strokes cut through his writhing, vicious, coward's courage, bit deeper, till at last, with a long whimper that became a yell, he went limp.

Ursula releases her hold on Williams at this point, but she sees his eyes and teeth "glinting" at her and thinks for a second with terror in her heart: "he was a beast thing." Then she grabs him again, "and the cane came down on him. A few times, madly, in a frenzy, he lunged and writhed, to kick her. But again the cane broke him, he sank with a howling yell on the floor, and like a beaten beast lay there yelling."

It is only here and now – "towards the end of this performance" – that Mr. Harby, the headmaster, rushes in from his own classroom to find out what the matter is. Ursula, feeling as if something were going to break in her, manages to force out with her last breath: "I've thrashed him." Looking at the writhing, howling figure on the floor, Ursula tells Williams to get up and stand by the room's radiator and, although he had been in "a mad frenzy," Williams – "with a little dart," his yelling dropped to "a mad blubber" – mechanically complies.

The headmaster continues to stand there, robbed of movement and speech while Ursula stands stiff not far from him: "Nothing could touch her now: she was beyond Mr. Harby. She was as if violated to death." The headmaster mutters something, turns, and returns in a rage to his own class.

No sooner has Headmaster Harby left then the game in Ursula's classroom resumes:

> The boy blubbered wildly by the radiator. Ursula looked at the class.
> There were fifty pale, still faces watching her, a hundred round eyes fixed
> on her in an attentive, expressionless stare.

Ursula tells her classroom monitors to give out the history books and assigns an in-class chapter of reading: "There was a click of many books opened. The children found the page, and bent their heads obediently to read. And they read, mechanically." Ursula, trembling violently, goes and sits in her high chair, as Williams continues to blubber:

> She sat still without moving, her eyes watching the class, unseeing. She
> was quite still, and weak. She felt that she could not raise her hand from
> the desk. If she sat there for ever, she felt she could not move again, nor
> utter a command. It was a quarter-past four. She almost dreaded the
> closing of the school, when she would be alone.

After a while, the tension in the classroom relaxes. Ursula tells Williams, who is still crying, to get back to his seat: "As he sat down, he glanced at her furtively, his eyes still redder. Now he looked like some beaten rat."

Finally, the school day is over and the children are gone. Mr. Harby treads by heavily, without looking in Ursula's direction, or speaking. Mr. Brunt, on the other hand – ever the veteran mentor to the novice teacher, his blue eyes glancing down in a strange fellowship, his long nose pointing at her – approaches and says to Ursula as she is locking up her classroom cupboard: "If you settle Clarke and Letts in the same way, Miss Brangwen, you'll be all right." Ursula laughs nervously, and not wanting anyone to talk to her says only, "Shall I?"

As Ursula goes down the street on the way to the tram that will take her home, she becomes aware of some boys dodging behind her. Something strikes her hand, the one with which she is carrying her handbag, and whatever the object might have been, it has bruised her hand; however, as the object rolls away on the ground, Ursula sees that it was a potato that was thrown at her. Her hand hurts, but she ignores the pain:

She was afraid, and strange. It was to her quite strange and ugly, like some dream where she was degraded. She would have died rather than admit it to anybody. She could not look at her swollen hand. Something had broken in her; she had passed a crisis. Williams was beaten, but at a cost.

Feeling too much upset to go home, she rode a little farther into the town, and got down from the tram at a small tea-shop. There, in the dark little place behind the shop, she drank her tea and ate bread-and-butter. She did not taste anything. The taking of tea was just a mechanical action, to cover over her existence. There she sat in the dark, obscure little place, without knowing. Only unconsciously she nursed the back of her hand, which was bruised.

When finally she took her way home, it was sunset red across the west. She did not know why she was going home. There was nothing for her there. She had, true, only to pretend to be normal. There was nobody she could speak to, nowhere to go for escape. But she must keep on, under this read sunset, alone, knowing the horror in humanity, that would destroy her, and with which she was at war. Yet it had to be so.

In the morning again she must go to school. She got up and went without murmuring even to herself. She was in the hands of some bigger, stronger, coarser will.

A commentary on "the war of the worlds" in Ursula Brangwen's classroom

Now that you have been through Ursula's and Williams's teaching and learning disaster and thought about its relevance to your own or future classroom, you might find it additionally valuable to compare your ideas and feelings with the kind of professional journal writing education majors have done on this "incident" when asked to do an extended analysis:

> *The excerpt from the 1915 novel* <u>The Rainbow</u> *begins with Ursula's decision to relinquish her humanity in order to "assert" mastery over her students. She had decided to engage in a power play, setting herself against her students. As a teacher, she feels she must overpower and subdue the will of her students. She is forced to take this step after several colleagues comment on her need to have control in the classroom if she is to teach. With no support and understanding, Ursula succumbs to this philosophy, which wrecks her as well.*

*The major scene in this text is between Ursula and one of her students,
Williams, whom she already sees as her "enemy," and as "cunning" and
"degenerate." Williams was a threat to Ursula because he could, by his example of
ridiculing or challenging the teacher's authority, goad his classmates to follow his
lead.*

*Ursula's "hardness," her artificial newly found sense of authority, can be
seen in the scene between her and Williams, a scene initiated by a trivial incident,
"a blot" on his composition. Whether or not it was a mistake, Ursula seizes this
"mistake" of Williams to punish him, requiring him to stay after school and do
his writing. The student resists her, writing very little. It is clear that he is insolent
and only half-heartedly following her direction.*

*Ursula does not have many options open to her which can help her deal
effectively with Williams. We as readers do not know why there is so much hatred
and mistrust between the two. She threatens Williams with a visit to Mr. Harby,
the headmaster, but even the headmaster himself couldn't bear to deal with him.*

*After he has bothered his classmates, Ursula calls on Williams to come in
front of the class and Williams voices a clear "I shan't." This is an attack of war,
and Ursula responds the only way she knows how. For her to be taken seriously
by the rest of the class, she has to put Williams in his place, and assert her power.
Thus, she grabs Williams and drags him in front of the class, while he struggles
and kicks her all the way. She grabs the cane and gives him a thrashing.*

*At this point we can see Ursula as a person devoid of all mercy, kindness,
and compassion. She is cold, calculating, and afraid. She is engaged with the
enemy and though his is a victim, in the scene, the writer depicts him as a beastlike
creature and not at all human. Throughout the scene he is referred to as "a mad
thing" that "writhes" and whimpers. He becomes "a beast thing," with teeth and
eyes "glinting." In this terrible scene Williams is totally dehumanized. Ursula
regains control of her classroom. Her students obediently begin their reading
assignment. There is absolute silence. Williams, "the beaten rat," is told to return
to his seat.*

*The toll this behavior has on Ursula is significant and large. She is totally
drained, weak. She feels like an automaton, mechanically having her tea. She was
herself wounded – something had broken in her. Though she had beaten Williams,
she had lost her beliefs, her hope in humanity. She was no longer in control of her
actions – she felt like she was in the "hands of some bigger, stronger, coarser will."*

*From that point on, Ursula had to be always on her guard. The class could
spring on her at any moment. She could not let her guard down or show any
weakness. Unfortunately, only at the point where she is able to defeat Williams
does Ursula gain professional recognition for "settling" Williams.*

*The excerpt poses a serious question. What should a teacher do when
he or she has a student like Williams, a student who defies authority, disrupts
instruction, and wages a "war" with the teacher?*

Today's teachers have to follow the school's code of conduct, which details measures involved in carrying disciplinary action against a student. The teacher can try and first talk to the student, try to find out the reasons behind the student's acting out, trying to see why the student is so needy of attention, in this case "negative attention."

Another step is to discuss the situation with the parent and perhaps have a parent-teacher-student conference in which a solution would be arrived at. The guidance counselor or social worker could be asked to spend time with this student and determine the causes for the disruptive/violent behavior.

In a school of "intimidating adults," this approach may not work. In this case a peer mediator committee could help out by having a hearing about the case. Perhaps hearing the information from his or her peers might strike home faster. I believe that to help such a student all the human services at the school's disposal must be utilized. Perhaps in that way the problems underlying the student's inappropriate behavior could be successfully addressed.

The author of <u>So You Think You Might Like to Teach</u> has called the chapter you just finished reading the "saddest" chapter of the eight that make up this book. How do you feel about his description?

7

Making the connection:
the gift of good teaching

T wo fictional secondary school teachers (and one fictional elementary school student who has somehow slipped herself in!) consider – philosophically and practically – different approaches to teaching and learning

Cast of Characters

E. R. Braithwaite, *from* <u>To Sir, With Love</u> *by E. R. Braithwaite, Great Britain, 1959*

Francie Nolan, *from* <u>A Tree Grows in Brooklyn</u> *by Betty Smith, United States, 1943 (Francie is an elementary school student advanced for her age who has slyly infiltrated this book featuring secondary school teachers)*

Ollie Marcus, *from* <u>If You Knew Me</u> *by Anne Roiphe, United States, 1993 (fictional teacher #22)*

Introduction to making a connection with your students

Although there is no teacher in E. M. Forster's novel *Howards End*, the key lesson this work of literature leaves its readers with is: "connect."

As a new teacher, you may be feeling that in your case this is easier said than done. And you're right. But it is a goal to never lose sight of: connect with your philosophy of education, connect with your teacher persona, connect with your subject, connect with your students. Be passionate in your teaching, and be compassionate with your students.

Because teaching is such difficult and demanding work in the service of others (and we're not even mentioning the paperwork and school politics, though apparently we are), it is not for everyone. Sometimes – or perhaps I should say "often" – the most passionate and compassionate teacher is the one to fall victim to burnout.

Particularly in your first year (or two) as a teacher, you may feel that you are simply "treading water" when what you wanted was to have all the strokes down right from the start. The bad news: it doesn't get a whole lot easier. The good news: it does get a whole lot better.

You will be happy to hear that your first couple of years as a teacher are your most important – as long as you recognize your mistakes and learn from them. Don't be too hard on yourself, and try not to take your professional setbacks personally. You're learning your profession by doing. You didn't enter the pool by walking through the shallow water; you've dived in at the deep end while others are watching poolside to see whether you'll surface. Your ears are water-clogged and you've swallowed chlorine but if, after every lesson you teach, you remain a student of your own teaching, you will have all that you need to swim – swimmingly – another day.

E. R. Braithwaite's desire to become the best possible teacher he can be

In this regard, the "inspired-by-actual-people-and-events" story of British teacher E. R. Braithwaite in the novel *To Sir, With Love* is particularly instructive. In fact, how Braithwaite works to become, day by day, the best possible teacher he can be is the novel's story. Fairly late in the narrative, Braithwaite demonstrates that he understands that a teacher must always be a continual learner when he explains to a colleague why he has not even thought about moving on to some so-called "better school."

His reason, he says, is that he's "only just begun teaching, you know, not more than a few months. It hardly seems enough to decide whether or not I'm really much good at it." And, he continues, "I may be able to get to terms with these kids, but it might be quite different with others. I think I ought to stay where I am and learn a little more about the job and my own abilities before I think of moving."

Early in the narrative, having completed his studies to become a teacher, Braithwaite is on his way to an officially promised "appointment" to a school where a teacher has suddenly quit – no advance notice, no warning. Knowing little about the school but badly needing the job, Braithwaite is prepared to accept the assigned position. However, when he goes to meet with the school's headmaster, Alex Florian, as a matter of form the headmaster unexpectedly says: "We're glad to have you. I hope that when you've had a chance to look at us you'll be just as pleased to stay."

Braithwaite, appreciating the direct welcome of the first sentence but surprised by the implied option of the second, hastens to reassure the headmaster: "Not much doubt about that, Sir." That sounds like the practical or politically correct response, but consider how you would react and respond if the principal of the school you had been "assigned" to as your first school proposed something like the following:

I think it would be best if you had a good look around the school first, and then we'll talk about it. Things are done here somewhat differently from the usual run, and many teachers have found it, shall we say, disquieting. Wander around just as you please, and see what's going on, and if you then decide to remain with us, we'll talk about it after lunch.

A commentary on wandering around a school here and now and wondering whether to accept a teaching position there and then

Wouldn't it be something if all new teachers had this option and opportunity? They might not wind up working in a school or department or for someone that they were philosophically or otherwise incompatible with.

As it turns out, Braithwaite, in fact, does find somewhat "disquieting" what he glimpses and overhears as he "wanders around." Nevertheless, because he desperately needs the job (having been repeatedly and blatantly discriminated against in England because of his skin color when he sought work as a communications engineer, his original vocation), Braithwaite accepts the appointment to a new career and begins teaching his class that very day.

Braithwaite's feeling "disquieted" is the result of a palpable *disconnect* between his attitude, experiences, and success as a student and what he sees and overhears as he has "a good look around." As he checks out a school building that he himself finds "depressing, like a prison," Braithwaite cannot help but compare his own experiences as a student with what he observes among the student body of what will be his first school as a teacher. In similar circumstances, you, too, would quite naturally compare and contrast, evaluate and judge the schools you've experienced as a student with those you are considering as a prospective teacher.

A brief aside – and it's elementary – from the other side of the teacher's desk from a "pupil" of education

In Betty Smith's novel *A Tree Grows in Brooklyn*, little Francie Nolan, growing up and attending elementary school in the Williamsburg section of Brooklyn early in the twentieth century, also has some thoughts and feelings about the school she attended as a young student. Amidst the "meanness" that Francie finds within the "cruel and ugly routine" of her grade school, Francie also discovers certain positives that her home life lacked.

Author Betty Smith tells us that Francie Nolan "liked school in spite of all the meanness, cruelty, and unhappiness. The regimented routine of many children, all doing the same thing at once, gave her a feeling of safety. She felt that she was a definite part of something, part of a community gathered under a leader for the one purpose . . . . Francie felt a certain safety and security in school. Although it was a cruel and ugly routine, it had a purpose and a progression." Do you have comparable feelings about your own elementary and secondary school experiences?

Are all comparisons odious? Comparing your days as a student with those of your students

For some of you as pupils and students, school was a second home (or, as for Francie Nolan, a safe and secure first home) – a structured place where you fit in, were accepted, and became your best self; the ordered workings of institutionalized school made that possible. School was also a place where as a result of your hard work you experienced both internal rewards (the joy of learning, the thrill of mastering material you realized you had come to love) and external rewards (good grades, school honors and awards, teacher acknowledgment and approval, admission to college). Perhaps your life as a student foretold your life as a teacher.

E. R. Braithwaite, like Francie Nolan, early on in the narrative of *To Sir, With Love* shares memories of his own student days. A black man born and reared in British Guiana, Braithwaite also compares these memories with what he sees and hears during his "good look around" his future school as a teacher – and the comparison leaves him depressed. He tells us: "My depression deepened and I thought how very different all this was from my own childhood schooldays spent in warm sunny Georgetown. There, in a large rambling wooden schoolhouse, light and cool within, surrounded by wide, tree-shaded lawns on which I had romped with my fellows in vigorous contentment, I spent rich, happy days, filled with the excitement of learning, each new little achievement a personal adventure and a source of satisfaction to my interested parents."

Braithwaite concludes this memory with two questions he has already implied an answer to: "How did these East London children feel about coming to this forbidding-looking place, day after day? Were they as eagerly excited about school as I had been when a boy?"

A commentary on "happy days, filled with the excitement of learning" juxtaposed with "this forbidding-looking place"

Braithwaite's two questions about his future students and their feelings about school are posed rhetorically; yet the fact that he asks them in the context of his own very positive school memories and calls the East London school building a "forbidding-looking place" strongly suggests the answers would be in the negative. Still, most of the teachers depicted in *To Sir, With Love*, we learn as the narrative continues, do right by their students – that unsuccessful teacher that Braithwaite replaces, notwithstanding.

Doing what you believe to be "right" by your students

But what does "doing right" by students consist of? How much of an intuitive understanding does Braithwaite demonstrate in his words and actions on Day 1 as he addresses his students for the first time? Standing in front of his desk, Braithwaite waits until the students have settled in their seats and tries "to inject as much pleasant informality as possible" into his voice: "The Headmaster," he begins "has told you my name, but it will be some little while before I know all yours, so in the meantime I hope you won't mind if I point at you or anything like that; it will not be meant rudely."

Braithwaite next shares his plan for the day: "I do not know anything about you or your abilities, so I will begin from scratch. One by one I'll listen to you reading; when I call your name will you please read anything you like from any one of your schoolbooks."

Braithwaite then adds in the same vein, "Our arithmetic lesson will be on weights and measures. As with our reading lesson, I am again trying to find out how much you know about it and you can help by answering my questions as fully as you are able."

Take a moment to *re-read the above scene* with the following questions in mind:

- *What significance do you attach to the fact that Braithwaite stands in front of – not behind – the teacher's desk and waits till his new students have settled in their seats before addressing them?*
- *How and where does Braithwaite demonstrate an understanding of the importance not only of assessment but also of explaining to his students the teaching rationale behind assessment?*
- *If you were an observer in Braithwaite's classroom evaluating him on how well he has tried to get off to a good start, which particular techniques would you identify as potentially effective? What reasons would you give to Braithwaite so that as a new teacher he would clearly understand both what makes his weaknesses weak and what makes his strengths strong?*

A commentary on how the journey of a thousand miles begins with one step – or one misstep

Although it would be natural for you to be curious about whether Braithwaite's first interactions with his class worked (for teaching and learning), you do not in reality need to know the "outcomes" of his efforts in order to evaluate their "potential." To begin with, Braithwaite has physically and symbolically removed a barrier and narrowed the distance between himself and his students by positioning himself in front of the teacher's desk. (Would it be better – the barrier of the teacher's desk still behind him – for Braithwaite to sit in a chair or desk-chair at student level? Some American teachers would say so.)

Braithwaite tells us that he purposely chose an informal tone of voice for his "first impression" on his students rather than a formal "address" with its connotation of "talking down from on high." Similarly, because he expects to receive respect from the members of his class Braithwaite *shows* them respect as human beings and as young adults.

Repeatedly, Braithwaite treats these adolescents like the true students he hopes they will become: he provides an educational explanation for the teaching procedure he plans to follow, one that will address their needs ("so I will begin from scratch"); he anticipates a possible negative misinterpretation of his pointing to students until he learns their names ("it will not be meant rudely"); he admits that he, too, is human ("it will take some while before I . . ."); he models good manners ("please," "I hope you won't mind"); and he communicates that he believes in giving students free choice within educationally sound limits ("read anything you like from any one of your schoolbooks").

Understanding the importance of assessment for the purposes of reviewing, reinforcing, and reteaching, Braithwaite proceeds to apply to an arithmetic assessment the same teaching procedure he used for an earlier reading assessment; this shows, in addition, that he recognizes an opportunity to make a meaningful connection between two "different" parts of the lesson ("I am again trying to find out how much you know").

Nevertheless, the key strength of Braithwaite's respectful opening conversation with his new students is that it *is* a conversation, not a formal lecture. His purpose is to let them know at the very start of their teacher-student relationship that not only does he want to help them but also that he understands that he needs *their* help (not just their co-operation) in order to be of any real *service* to them as people with lives and futures ("and you can help by . . .").

The three phases of E. R. Braithwaite's approach to his students

Clearly, on his first day as their teacher, Braithwaite strives to convey to his students that he is human and that his heart is in the right place. With the passing of time, Braithwaite's teaching style and his relationship with his students passes through three distinct phases. "I tried very hard to be a successful teacher with my class," he tells us, "but somehow, as day followed day in painful procession, I realized that I was not making the grade."

As you move with Braithwaite through these three phases, what would you say Braithwaite is learning about being a "successful" teacher? Is this new knowledge applicable elsewhere – to other students in other schools (and to other teachers like yourself)? What else, would you say, does Braithwaite need to learn?

In Phase 1, Braithwaite's students would give him "the silent treatment," and "during that time, for my first few weeks, they would do any task I set them without question or protest, but equally without interest or enthusiasm; and if their interest was not required on the task in front of them they would sit and stare at me with the same careful, patient attention a birdwatcher devotes to the rare feathered visitor . . . . It made me nervous and irritable, but I kept a grip on myself" and "took great pains with the planning of my lessons, using illustrations from the familiar things of their own background . . . . I created varying problems within the domestic framework, and tried to encourage their participation, but it was as though there was a conspiracy of disinterest, and my attempts at informality fell pitifully flat."

In the second "and more annoying phase of their campaign," Braithwaite's students would give him "the noisy treatment"; for example, when Braithwaite would speak or read aloud "someone would lift the lid of a desk and let it fall with a loud bang; the culprit would merely sit and look at me with wide innocent eyes as if it were an accident. They knew as well as I did that there was nothing I could do about it, and I bore it with as much a show of aplomb as I could manage. One or two such interruptions during a lesson was usually enough to destroy its planned continuity, and I was often driven to the expedient of . . . substituting some form of written work; they could not write and bang their desks at the same time."

Also during the noisy treatment phase, Braithwaite could not talk as much with the class "about everything and anything"; the bell would less frequently find teacher and students "deep in interested discussion," with Braithwaite "showing them that the whole purpose of their education was the development of their own thinking and reasoning."

By Phase 3, "there was growing up between the children and myself a real affection which I found very pleasant and encouraging. Each day I tried to present to them new facts in a way which would excite and stimulate their interest, and gradually they were developing a readiness to comment and also a willingness to tolerate the expressed opinions of others; even when those opinions were diametrically opposed to theirs . . . . I was learning from them as well as teaching them. I learned to see them in relation to their surroundings, and in that way to understand them."

A commentary on good teaching: it's "a gift"

Most people would agree that "giving" is a good thing – and "gifted" teachers make a present of their expertise every day. This is the gift that never stops giving because through inquiry and discovery it empowers students to gain knowledge and achieve understanding. Good teaching on the high school and college levels may, in fact, have inspired *you* to think about becoming a teacher. Good teaching is in evidence whenever students can be seen and heard using their minds, getting practice with the process, and coming to understand how they and other individuals think.

Learning through inquiry and discovery is a habit that needs to be consciously developed over time in order to eventually become sub-consciously second nature. Students need to *listen to* and *hear* themselves and others explain their thinking processes about the content of a subject area so that they can identify "reasonable" patterns of circuitry and instances of short-circuitry. That's what being "a student" of social studies, or science, or English, or math should be about.

It is critically important for those teachers with students who do not enter the classroom excited about learning that these students at least be traveling on the road toward excitement when they leave each day. Teachers who disproportionately favor the lecture method of instruction are usually trying to "cover" the material *for* their students. They do this by cramming as many facts and *teacher* insights as possible into their students' heads in the administratively allotted period of time. Students are passively left to get excited about the teacher's excitement – if, in fact, the teacher is genuinely excited.

The tests that assess this kind of learning, whether standardized or teacher-created, reward students for their memories – their ability to "recover" through recall enough of the exact material the teacher has "covered" in order to pass. This is achievable – but what kind of achievement does it represent? If you think about what a "cover" does, you should have second thoughts about an educational practice that brings to mind images of "hiding from sight." Besides, within days after a "regurgitation"-type test, most students' memories are back to being almost blank.

Good teaching practices the art of questioning (attention paid to both content and wording) with the teacher functioning as inciter, motivator, exciter, stimulator, instigator, intriguer, provoker, challenger, and disturber. "Incite" questions and their like seek to provoke student "insights" by *prompting* the really hard work of thinking. "Re-covering" of relevant and significant facts is always in the service of that quest.

Are there prefixes other than "re-" that can be affixed to the word "cover" in order to capture better educational practices than "covering" and "recovering" the material? Like the archeologist on a dig, students engaged in real thinking need to "**un**cover" material before they can make connections and "**dis**cover" (infer, conclude) something of consequence in a particular subject area and to themselves and their lives. In short, students need to dig before they can "dig" it.

When teachers "cover" the material for their students, they are merely sharing someone else's archeological-type discovery, and if they stop short of challenging their students to reflect on possible or probable relationships and patterns, then "the dig" will soon get "covered over" in most students' minds.

Connecting with another person "as if you knew me"

Before you look at a very brief excerpt from Anne Roiphe's novel *If You Knew Me*, it is important to note that it is not being presented here as a model lesson from a model lesson plan. Nor is it an example of questioning at its best.

Instead, it is offered for your consideration as an attempt on the part of high school English teacher Ollie Marcus to keep his teenage students reading, reacting to, and connecting with a classic work of American literature, *as if they actually knew the characters*. The hope would be that in subsequent lessons, key themes and authorial artistry could then be more fully and insightfully explored.

The lesson deals with Nathaniel Hawthorne's *The Scarlet Letter*, a novel that many American high school students *unthinkingly* reject as "irrelevant" to their lives. From the perspective of a teacher of any subject, what do you find positive about the lesson? Similarly, what do you find positive from a student's perspective? Finally, where do these two perspectives converge for you as someone who has just started to or might like to teach?

Connecting as presented in _If You Knew Me_

Ollie Marcus said to his class, Who is innocent in this book?
Bruce Holloway said, Big deal, she slept with the minister.
Ollie said, Should she have been punished?
Ellen said, They should have punished him, not her.
Ollie said, He did it alone?
Mary Harden, blushing, said, Sometimes people love each other, and you do things you shouldn't.
Ollie said, There are no consequences? You don't pay for your acts?
Ellen said, It was cruel, the letter *A* was cruel.
Ollie said, Cruel, let's talk about cruel.

In a comparable lesson that Ollie Marcus teaches about the arguably even more student-rejected American classic novel, *Moby Dick*, by Herman Melville, author Anne Roiphe writes at the beginning of her account of the lesson: "Ollie talked to his class. 'The fish, what was it? What do you think?' A hand went up." At the end of the lesson, "Ollie said, 'Were you sad at the end?' The class considered. The bell rang."

A commentary on keeping the classroom "conversation" going through teacher follow-up questioning and student connecting

It is not accidental that author Anne Roiphe introduces each of these lessons from a high school English class with a conversational verb: "Ollie *said* to his class"; "Ollie *talked* to his class." In each lesson, teacher Ollie Marcus is initiating a possible conversation with and among his students; he is not commencing a "canned" lecture. Intentionally, Marcus's interjections into the conversation once it begins are concise gently probing questions. Perhaps he fears that anything more obviously teacher-sounding would shut the students down.

Today's literature study teachers daily dip into their arsenal of follow-up questions and pull out such highly effective one-word and short-phrase follow-up questions as "So?" and "Well?" and "What's the big deal?" Like Marcus's small talk questions about serious matters, their purpose is to keep the conversation going. As long as that happens, even the most private students continue to have an opportunity to *connect* with important ideas and feelings inherent in the material and with one another's lives. As E. M. Forster wrote: "connect."

Of course, Marcus's larger pedagogical aim is to make it possible for his students to come to the realization (to "discover") that what makes these two classic nineteenth-century novels "classic" is that they continue to "speak to" a whole range of emotional and intellectual concerns that are universal and timeless. Another "connection."

These human concerns in Marcus's classroom mean the concerns of Bruce, and Ellen, and Mary, and Martha, and Alan ("who hardly ever said anything"), and Mark, and Howard. "The class *considered*" – and that's a start. Still another "connection" has been made.

Students who are becoming good thinkers often realize quite early that good thinking is at its best when it includes *thinking about thinking* – the thinking process both around them in the classroom and inside them as students. Good thinkers have learned that the "sudden" thought is the concluding "speck" on the process of linear thought.

When a class of students "considers" the content and wording of a teacher's carefully crafted thought-provoking questions, as well as the student-to-student questions of their classmates and their own "I-just-thought-of-it" questions as stimulated by "conversation," there is no more exciting place in the world than that classroom, no matter what the subject matter.

To help students learn about the thinking process (which is the same process at the core of many kinds of academic writing and the reason those kinds of writing are so difficult for many students), a teacher in any subject area is always a teacher of critical thinking about that subject.

Some examples of the kinds of things that good thinkers try to do with any content – and that all teachers across the disciplines can model and teach

- ask questions;
- recognize that there are things that they don't know;
- admit it when they don't know something;
- admit it when they are not sure of something;
- try to find out as much information as possible before forming an opinion;
- keep an open mind to new ideas and other people's points of view;
- have a genuine interest in other people's opinions;
- realize that what *they* think is obvious is not always obvious to others, or to any single individual all the time;
- base their ideas and opinions on a knowledge of established facts;
- think about why they think what they think (have reasons for their ideas and viewpoints);
- think about how they came to think what they think (think about the act and process of thinking);
- tend to be skeptical in a way that is not off-putting or confrontational;
- understand the difference between things that are possible, things that are probable, and things that are certain or definite (for the time being);
- try to be aware of their assumptions (first realizing that they are bound to have some);
- make a periodic point of re-examining their assumptions.

Some examples of the kinds of things that good thinkers try to avoid doing whatever the content – and that students can learn to unlearn

- open their mouths before they open their minds (the "knee-jerk" equivalent for the mouth – a "jaw-jerk");
- take a side in a disagreement and stay loyal to it no matter what (as is expected in a formal debate, where winning the debate, not necessarily finding out the truth, is the goal);
- think they know it all (and come across to others as a "know-it-all");
- think that others don't know anything;
- close their minds to new ideas and different points of view;
- take things for granted;
- never question their beliefs;
- fail to distinguish between belief and knowledge;
- take on faith matters that need to be factually examined;
- allow their emotions to rule their thinking;

- view other people and situations through bias or prejudice;
- let others do their thinking for them.

In the very real world of school, even the best and brightest students, our most insightful and creative thinkers, have much to learn, and they deserve to be *motivated* to learn to their fullest potential and satisfaction. Relying on any student to be "self-motivated" is at best a rationalization and at worst a cop-out.

In *To Sir, With Love*, it is only after a mutual "give-and-take" during the third and final phase of Braithwaite's relationship with his far-from-self-motivated students that Braithwaite is viewed by his class as "sir – with love." When those words appear for the first time – on the final page of the novel – Braithwaite knows he has earned all that that tribute implies. Whatever your feelings about the salaries teachers make, the answer to the question *What do teachers "make"?* is that good teachers "make" a difference.

Unfortunately, so do less than satisfactory teachers. It is both naïve and uniformed to believe that if students come to school eager to learn, or are naturally bright, or are hard-working, not even the worst teacher can keep them from learning. Most of us who have conducted supervisory visits to America's classrooms in recent years would argue that that belief sells bad-teaching short. Don't underestimate the power of poor teaching to undercut and undermine learning even among the most self-motivated of students.

Sometimes, when these ineffective teachers are asked to explain certain poor teaching practices, they get defensive and insist that they are under pressure "to *cover* the material." To put it bluntly, the only thing these teachers are covering is their posteriors. And, thanks to the practice of random programming of many high school students, some of these teachers may be currently teaching the students that *you* will inherit next year.

How's that for a gift?

8

From "Teacher, know thyself"
to "Self, how'm I doin'?"

A *final case study of one semi-fictional urban American high school teacher – from lesson plan to lesson execution to student assessment to official supervisory observation to informal evaluation*

Cast of Characters

Sylvia Barrett, *from* <u>Up the Down Staircase</u> *by Bel Kaufman, United States, 1964; this concluding chapter of* **So You Think You Might Like to Teach** *is different from the preceding seven in that it does all it needs to do with* **only one fictional teacher**, *#23 of the book's subtitle – and it does this by looking at some traditional documents in this and every other teacher's career: the teacher's formal lesson plan; class minutes written by a student (for the benefit of absentees and "cutters") in which the teaching of the missed lesson is discussed; and informal observation notes from the teacher's subject supervisor, who was officially present for the teaching of the lesson.*

Introduction to the novel <u>Up the Down Staircase</u>

The title of this semi-autobiographical novel is world famous (please don't call it "Staircase," even informally!) because one of the things it has come to represent around the globe is the idea that in a-less-than-"ideal" urban school, students will generally pay no mind to an attempt to capture actual and symbolic "order" with stairwell signs for ascending and descending; the resulting interweaving of students will not be chaos or confusion but the lively and rebellious diversity of real life in a real world.

As author Bel Kaufman wrote in explaining the title in connection with the 25th anniversary edition of <u>Up the Down Staircase</u>*: "In those days there were UP and DOWN signs on narrow school stairs to facilitate traffic.* <u>Up the Down Staircase</u> *stood for the* *pettiness of administration; at the same time, it was a metaphor for going against traffic, bucking the system."*

Author Kaufman adds that she was originally *"worried"* that the title *"sounded too clumsy and unwieldy"* and that she could not help but wonder: *"How would anyone remember it?"* Go figure! (The title of Neil Postman's and Charles Weingartner's pioneering 1969 non-fiction work calling for a *"new education"* for new times similarly echoes the transformative importance of *"bucking the system"*: <u>Teaching as a Subversive Activity</u>; their book remains an important one for starting-out teachers to know.)

Teachers teach and students learn, but at any given moment, are the students learning what the teachers are teaching or think they are teaching?

Lessons exist first on paper – in the potential of the lesson plan. Later, in actuality, they exist in the practice of the teacher. And, ultimately, they exist in the pupils – in the particular minds and hearts of the students present in the classroom. Would each of these several lessons recognize one another?

Teachers who talk to themselves – and all good teachers do – are certain to have that internal conversation that goes something like this: "Here's what I had hoped to teach. Here's what I think I taught. Now, what did each of my students learn?"

In the semi-autobiographical novel *Up the Down Staircase*, brand-new high school English teacher Sylvia Barrett (reflecting author Bel Kaufman's experience in a New York City high school) plans a literature study lesson for her thirty-nine students (yes, 39! it's the late 1950's in an urban high school) on the well-known poem "The Road Not Taken" – and in her execution of the lesson, she is formally observed by her subject supervisor.

You may want to reference this highly anthologized Robert Frost poem but is not really essential to what this concluding chapter hopes to examine, in general, about teaching and learning across most major subject areas on the secondary level.

Three documents *will* be essential – and they are provided unabridged and unedited; the first (below) is the "Model Outline of Lesson Plan" prepared by Miss Barrett for her poetry lesson; the second document (which follows almost immediately) is a written summary and assessment of the lesson – not by Miss Barrett's supervisor, which is what you might have been expecting – but by a student in the class for the benefit of any absentees upon their return to class; and the third document (much further along in the chapter) is made up of unofficial notes from Miss Barrett's subject supervisor on the lesson he observed her teach (but *not* his written formal observation report, which, again, is what you might have been expecting).

Certain aspects of Miss Barrett's "model outline of lesson plan" may look strange to you and certain concepts and terminology she makes use of may seem foreign or unfamiliar (depending on what part of the country you were schooled in, the decades that have passed since this plan was created, and your particular subject area); as an aid to understanding, try to come up with possible equivalents from your own experiences in education courses, student teaching, or any regular teaching you have done.

As you review Miss Barrett's lesson plan, consider (by doing the following) its pedagogical strengths and weaknesses from the point of view of her 39 students and from the point of view of her observing supervisor:

- Pretend you are a student of Miss Barrett's who was either absent from or was cutting (your choice!) her poetry lesson. What of significance would you say you missed learning that day in English class (based solely on the written plan)?
- Pretend you are Miss Barrett's subject supervisor (and, therefore, her mentor) and give her some informal pointers on which aspects of her written plan constitute good planning for a potentially successful lesson and which aspects need to be revised – and why.

Sylvia Barrett's "Model Outline of Lesson Plan"

1. **Topic**: "The Road Not Taken" by Robert Frost
2. **Aim**: Understanding and appreciation of the poem
3. **Motivation**: Interesting, challenging, thought-provoking questions, relating to the students' own experiences
    1. What turning point have *you* had in your life?
    2. What choice did you make, and why?
    3. How did you feel about your choice later?
4. **Anticipation of difficulties**: Put on board and explain words: *diverged, trodden*
5. **Factual content of lesson**: Read the poem aloud: "Two roads diverged in a yellow wood . . ." etc.
6. **Pivotal questions; directed towards appreciation of human motives**:
    1. Why did he make this particular choice of road?
    2. Why does he say: "I shall be telling this with a sigh"? What kind of sigh will it be? One of regret? Relief?
    3. This poem ends with: "I took the one less traveled by, And that has made all the difference." *What* difference do you suppose it made to him?
    4. Had he taken the *other* road, how would the poem have ended? (Elicit from them: The same way!)
    5. Why does Frost call it "The Road Not Taken" rather than "The Road Taken"? (Elicit: We regret things we haven't done more than those we have.)

6. Based on this poem, what kind of person do you suppose Frost was?
    (Elicit: direct, simple, philosophical, man who loved nature and had
    an eye for concrete detail)
7. What is his style of writing? ("multum in parvo" or "much in little":
    economy of language, yet scope of thought)

7. **Enrichment:** Pass around photo of Frost.
8. **Summary:**

    1. Blazing a trail vs. conformity.
    2. Regret inherent in any decision.

(**Note**: Remember summary on *board!*
    Windows!
    No paper scraps on floor!
    Try to get Eddie Williams to recite at least once.
    Don't let Harry Kagan do all the talking.
    Change Linda's seat – put her next to girl?
    If time, play record of Frost reading own poetry.)

A commentary on "the road planned" for the class by the teacher – and how it compares with the actual trip the students took

When Sylvia Barrett gets advance notice that her English supervisor will formally observe her teach a particular class on a scheduled day, she wonders what kind of lesson she should plan for the occasion. You might knowingly smile were you to read in *Up the Down Staircase* that one of Miss Barrett's more veteran colleagues advises her to give a full-period test, while another recommends that she have the students write in class on an assigned topic for the entire time. These colleagues were no doubt kidding (mostly), but they were also empathizing with a new teacher's natural fear of being visited, observed, evaluated, and judged.

Wisely, Miss Barrett's opts to actively teach, understanding that only in the process of teaching will she give her supervisor an opportunity to discover her strengths and weaknesses and make specific recommendations for her continued growth and development. In short, to mentor.

Incidentally, an astute observer of a full-period exam or writing activity would still be able to confer with the teacher on the strengths and weaknesses of the "lesson." For example, the supervisor might instructively ask about the strengths and weaknesses of the test or writing activity, whether it deserved the full period, what exactly the teacher had done to prepare the students for success on the test or with the writing, or what the teacher did of value during the time allotted to the students for the particular activity. (Can you think of other conference questions you might ask as a supervisor under these conditions?)

From the outline Miss Barrett goes on to create, it would also seem that she understands that the lesson she should plan and teach "for the occasion" should actually be the kind of lesson she would normally teach "for her students." It would be naïve to think that teachers who know ahead of time that their supervisor will be visiting will not include some "bells and whistles." So, you should not feel too guilty if you wind up doing just a bit of the same when your "boss" comes to call (particularly for the first time).

However, the key thing about your observation lesson is that it must be all about who you are as a teacher and who your students are as a class. The more real you are in your plan and its execution, the more of real value you will learn from your supervisor's follow-up.

Not so incidentally, a particularly loud "bell or whistle" will not go unnoticed and uncommented on by your supervisor ("Why did you do that?," "Is that something you do on a regular basis?," "When was the last time you . . . . ?"). More embarrassing still would be having students during the lesson question your innovative "bell" or "whistle" during the course of the lesson, puzzled by why you've done or asked something you've never done or asked before!

Many of you will probably point out that Miss Barrett's plan is almost as noteworthy for what it doesn't contain as for what it does. Let's mention but three of these items: individual student writing within the lesson, collaborative learning through group work, students' reading aloud of the poem. But we also need to acknowledge the fact that for most mid-twentieth century high school English teaching in the United States, the presence of these concepts in a teacher's plan and lesson was rare if not unheard of.

Miss Barrett has good intentions "if time" permits to "play record of Frost reading own poetry," but that activity is clearly optional and we are left to make our own inferences as to why she would think this would be a good teaching technique to consider but not one with high priority for this poem and this lesson. More noticeable by its absence is the fact that the teacher has not planned to have students read any lines of the poem aloud, something that could promote both individual and class comprehension through oral recitation and focused listening. (Miss Barrett's "note" to herself at the end of the plan to "try to get Eddie Williams to recite at least once" is not about Eddie's practicing his poetry reading aloud before an audience of his classmates but about his overall lack of participation in Miss Barrett's English class.)

The word "recite" might also make us wonder whether Miss Barrett sees the discussion of the poem as students' providing the *right answers* to her questions rather than their sharing of the critical thinking her "pivotal" questions provoke. Miss Barrett's three parenthetical uses of "elicit" could be seen in this context to mean something as teacher-centered as "go for and get this response as the right answer so that I, as teacher, will know that my students 'get' the poem."

Let's hope, instead, that by "elicit" Miss Barrett means something like the following stream of consciousness: "this pivotal question, when applied by my students to actual lines in the text, will lead them to articulate reasoned interpretations that are justifiable by the content, as opposed to student interpretations that, the class would agree, cannot be supported by the words of the poem either directly or inferentially."

Let's see where Miss Barrett's lesson plan actually takes us, careful to be alert to more than a half-century of changing terminology reflecting educational fashions that became trends, trends that became philosophy, and philosophy that became dogma. Did "aim" mean to Miss Barrett in the 1950's and 1960's what it might mean to you now in your current education course, or site school, or home school?

By "aim," Miss Barrett seems to have in mind the general goal or overall purpose of having her students come to an understanding and appreciation of a particular poem. (Perhaps in her heart Miss Barrett might harbor the hope that some of her students will actually wind up "getting" and liking "The Road Not Taken" enough to be both more open to and ready for the next poem she plans to teach, or even better, that they choose to read on their own.)

Realistically, Miss Barrett's lesson plan reveals an awareness of her students' possible mixed feelings about poetry in general. Her "motivation" activity is an attempt to overcome negative student assumptions about any poem's relevance to their lives; strategically, she plans to first engage her students with intriguing questions that thematically connect their world to the world of the poem. Only afterwards, in the body of the lesson, will she re-introduce similarly worded questions as the basis for an analysis of the poem.

This kind of "external" motivation (an opening question, or quotation, or brief written activity *seemingly* outside the actual text or specific content under study) continues to be a popular way for many subject area teachers to "hook" students on the body of the lesson to follow. When external motivations are made up of interesting, well-worded questions, intriguing statements, or challenging activities, a class can be moved smoothly and relatively quickly from a personal discussion of ideas to the content area's consideration of them. Relevance ("relatedness" or "identification" for those of you who may not like the term "relevance"), genuine interest, and real curiosity are established by the best external motivations.

In the hoped-for execution of Miss Barrett's poetry lesson, students not only will have been motivated to make the transition to the poem itself but also will be interested in seeing in some detail how the life of the poem connects with their own. *A caution:* unless this transition is made smoothly, efficiently, and honestly, students are reluctant to move from their own more narrowly defined personal interests to the lesson's larger and more universal content development; in fact, they may come to view external motivation as at best an overused gimmick and at worst a manipulative trick.

Academically versed in the subject matter content of her lesson (this particular poem, the life and body of work of the poet Robert Frost, the nature of poetry historically and currently), Miss Barrett appears to have included in her transition preliminary attention to possible obstacles to understanding: "anticipation of difficulties."

Teachers of all content areas can appreciate the importance of anticipating comprehension problems by teaching in advance such areas as key vocabulary, factual content, and difficult concepts and by sometimes having material read aloud well by the teacher, by selected students, and through professional recordings.

Within the body of her lesson plan, Miss Barrett would want to make certain to include a sequential and, usually, timed "procedure" or "development." (Many teachers today prefer the label "development" because it not only shows the sequenced procedure being followed but also states or implies, step by step, how the development's questions and activities build on and lead into one another.)

In item number 6 of her plan, we find that Miss Barrett refers to "pivotal" questions; this may date her now in some sections of the country and in certain educational circles, but the idea behind the term "pivotal questions" is instructive; hence, a definitional digression: a pivot is a small pin or bar that supports a larger object and lets it turn or swing. Pivotal questions, by their very name, should cause the lesson to move in the general direction of its planned goal through a series of zigs and zags: each of these turning movements (at their respective turning points) swings the lesson in the specific direction of the next pivot while all the time moving the lesson in the general direction of its final destination.

Effective planning requires the creation of a limited number of thought-provoking questions, key questions that will cause the exploration of the lesson's content to move students sequentially toward greater understanding and deeper insight. Without a doubt, the better the planned wording of a lesson's pivotal questions – and of the wording of the teacher's follow-up questions during the course of the class's student-to-student-student discussion – the better the chance that the lesson, when concluded, will have achieved its purpose.

Not accidentally, Miss Barrett's pivotal questions hark back to the thematic content and wording of her motivating questions. Students will now have to build on their initial conversation by including the viewpoints of found in the poem. Where the lesson's motivation involved personal talk about a "turning point" in an individual student's life, the lesson's development will require students to make references to actual visual images and word choices in the language of the poem, such as the quoted "I took the one less traveled by, And that has made all the difference."

Both this lesson's motivation and development make purposeful use of questions about the choices that life presents and about a person's later feelings about those choices. In fact, one of Miss Barrett's parenthetical "elicit" reminders to herself, pivotal question number 5 in her plan, requires students to consider the difference in meaning between two choices for the poem's title: the poem's actual title – "The Road Not Taken" – and a possible substitution: "The Road Taken."

One key insight the teacher hopes will be discovered and elicited ("drawn out") about man's choices in life is that "we regret things we haven't done more than those we have" but, as the teacher's "summary" states, there is "regret inherent in any decision," whether it is the more or less conventional one. A challenging question like this, in fact, might be saved for the last seven to ten minutes of the lesson (about the same amount of time allotted to the opening motivation), as it would make an excellent learning assessment question to conclude the class's discussion and assess the students' achievement of the lesson's aim.

Sylvia Barrett's plan ends with some other notes to herself: a mix of the seemingly administrative and purposefully pedagogical. The three that mention a student's name are all in the service of getting more students attentive to and involved in the class's discussion. (Harry Kagan is the "fastest hand in the class" and can monopolize the conversation. Linda, something of a flirt, may need to be seated away from boys in order to draw her attention to the lesson.)

The two notes that deal with the physical condition of the classroom – windows, paper scraps on floor – reflect areas Miss Barrett has been cautioned about by administrators. To put the best possible interpretation on things, we might hope that "windows" is code for "maintaining comfortable temperatures conducive to wide-awake listening, thinking and active participating" and that the concern about a clean classroom comes from the belief that it models a respect for education that includes where it occurs.

Before we go on to the reaction of Miss Barrett's visiting supervisor, Dr. Samuel Bester, to the lesson she actually taught from this plan, we have an opportunity to hear from one of the students present. This next excerpt from *Up the Down Staircase* is in the form of minutes on the period of instruction "respectfully submitted" by class secretary Janet Amdur, to be read aloud the next day for the benefit of absentees.

Mulling over the minutes

- *What are the strengths and weaknesses of Miss Barrett's poetry lesson as experienced by this particular student? Compare and contrast them with your own earlier thinking and the subsequent commentary on the lesson as planned.*
- *"How'm I doin'?" and "How are the students doing?" If you, as Miss Barrett's supervisor and mentor, had interviewed this fairly literate student in order to gain some educational insights into her observations, perceptions, understandings "learnings," emphases, and misconceptions, what, specifically, would you make a point of* communicating *to the teacher in a post-observation conference?*

- *As Miss Barrett's supervisor and mentor, what key recommendations for Miss Barrett's teaching – of a poem, of English, of language arts, of literature,* of any subject – *would you make certain to include in your* written *report? Explain the reasoning behind your recommendations.*

That day's class minutes

Dear Miss Barrett,

I'll be absent tomorrow due to sickness so please let some one else read these minutes I took on today's lesson.

It was a most interesting and educational English period. Miss Barrett collected money for the *Scholastics* and any one who doesn't bring it tomorrow won't get it. Miss Barrett read some notices about the G.O. and Mr. McHabe came in to speak about no sneakers on cafeteria tables. Miss Barrett sent Roy out of the room for spitting out of the window to cure hiccups and thought (sic) us a beautiful poem by Mr. Robert Frost. The title was called "The Road Not Taken." Dr. Bester visited us. He sat next to Fred.

We discussed our different turning points in life. Vivian's turning point was college or work after graduation? This was not a good example because she is only a soph. Linda's turning point was about which dress to wear Sat. night. Eddie's turning point was when he went to the cellar and got hit on the head. Lou had no turning point.

The poet tries to say that because he took the road this made a lot of difference. He tells about yellow wood. He decides to take a walk and takes a wrong turning point and gets lost and sighs. The moral is we can't walk on two roads at the same time. Some people in class disagreed.

The poet (Mr. Frost) teaches us about life and other things. He was simple. He was economical and died recently. He blazed a trial (sic) on a new road.

Miss Barrett passed around his picture but it got only to the first row because some wise guy hogged it and wouldn't pass it. Multim (sic) im (sic) parva (sic) means he says very little. Trodden means walk.

His style was very good. He had his eye on things.

In my last term's English class we had to put poems under different Headings like Poems of Love and Friendship, or Nature and God's Creatures, or Religion and Death, and say where they belong to, but I'm not sure where this one belong to.

Respectfully submitted,
Janet Amdur, Class Secretary

A commentary – in part from Miss Barrett – on one student's "most interesting and educational English period"

Soon after her teaching of "The Road Not Taken," Sylvia Barrett writes in a letter to her non-teacher friend Ellen that during her formal observation by her supervisor, she "taught a poem. Or did I?" Despite what she calls her "careful paper-plans" and despite some positive informal feedback from her supervisor (more about this soon), Miss Barrett concludes: "I don't think I got through to them."

What Miss Barrett says next in her letter gives us her take on the difference between what she planned to teach, what she might have thought she taught, and what one particular student "got" from the lesson in which Miss Barrett "taught a poem."

Of her students Miss Barrett writes: "The trouble is their utter lack of background. 'I never read a book in my life, and I ain't starting now,' a boy informed me. It isn't easy to make them like a book – other teachers got there before me." (She mentions a couple of her English teacher colleagues by name before she wonders, "Or perhaps it goes further back, to the 1st grade, or the 5th?")

Having reflected on where her students are coming from, Miss Barrett proceeds to formulate for her friend what she wants for their future – both in *her* English class and beyond:

> The important thing is to make them feel King Lear's anguish, not a True-or-False test on Shakespeare. The important thing is the recognition and response, not an inch of print to be memorized. I want to point the way to something that should forever lure them, when the TV set is broken and the movie is over and the school bell has rung for the last time.

A second reading of her student's minutes – a closer professional reading from a greater emotional distance – might provide Miss Barrett with some reassurance that both her heart and a good part of her mind were in the right place. Class secretary Janet Amdur, who says she found the lesson to be "a most interesting and educational English period," shows some insight, for instance, into the strengths and weaknesses of her classmates' examples of life's turning points in the lesson's motivating discussion.

However, Janet's understanding (but not her appreciation!) of what the poet "teaches" in "The Road Not Taken" about "life and other things" appears a bit shaky – though she is on firm ground when she says that "we can't walk on two roads at the same time." And although Janet adds that "some people in class disagreed," this very disagreement tells us that at least some students were listening to one another, thinking, speaking their minds, and, it is to be hoped, explaining why they thought the way they did based on lines from the poem.

Perhaps best of all for Janet's thinking and future understanding is her sharing of her reflective confusion about which category "heading" to place this particular poem under: "I'm not sure where this one belongs to." (Cherish and cultivate the student who begins an expressed thought with words like "I don't know but . . . .")

Huh? Where's the formal written observation report?

In *Up the Down Staircase*, Bel Kaufman does not give Miss Barrett's language arts supervisor's observations and perspective on the lesson by reprinting his formal (and official) evaluative report; instead, similar to Janet's minutes and Miss Barrett's letter to her friend Ellen, she shares an unofficial letter from Chairman Samuel Bester containing his commendations and recommendations.

Although Dr. Bester says his letter's twelve suggestions will not appear in his formal report, any student teacher or brand-new teacher who has had the opportunity to read a formal observation report would have to *wonder why not* when it comes to several of his recommendations. Are the reasons educational? Professional? Personal? Political?

We, of course, could speculate on the reasons (go ahead if you'd like), but let's also – for the sake of the teaching/learning value of *continuity of supervision* – decide which of Chairman Bester's suggestions *should be recorded by him in writing* so that Miss Barrett could refer to them between observations as she works to implement recommendations and to habitualize commendations.

Dr. Bester's Dozen

From: Samuel Bester, Chairman, Language Arts Dept.
To: Miss S. Barrett, Room 304

Miss Barrett,

The following suggestions are unofficial: they will not appear on my formal Observation Report. If you wish a personal conference, please see me.

1. Windows should be open about 4 inches *from the top*, to avoid danger of students leaning out.
2. Relating questions to the pupils' own experiences is first rate, but don't let them run away with you. They often do it to delay or

avoid a lesson. Example: in connection with making a choice, the discussion of whether or not a girl in 4^(th) row should wear her print or her green chiffon Saturday night was interesting, but 6 minutes on it was excessive.

3. Don't allow one student (Kagan?) to monopolize the discussion. Call on non-volunteers too.

4. Always ask the question first; then only call on a student by name, thus engaging the whole class in thinking. Avoid elliptical, loaded or vague questions, such as: "How do you feel about this poem?" (too vague) and "Do we regret what we haven't done?" (The answer the teacher wants must *obviously* be *yes!*)

5. Your unfailing courtesy to the students is first rate. A teacher is frequently the only adult in the pupil's environment who treats him with respect. Instead of penalizing suspended boy who came in late, with toothpick in mouth, you made him feel the class had missed his contribution to it. That's first rate! (He should, however, have been made to remove the toothpick.)

6. "Note the simplicity of Frost's language," you said. You might try the excellent device of pretending ignorance or surprise: "But I thought a poem had to have fancy words!" or "But isn't an adverb supposed to end in *ly*?" or "But doesn't Mark Antony say *nice* things about Brutus?"

7. The boy next to me was doing his math. It is wise for the teacher to move about the room.

8. Immediate correction of English was effected. However, you missed: "He should of took the road . . ." "On this here road . . ." "He *coont* make up his mind."

9. Enthusiasm is contagious. I'm glad you're not ashamed to show you are moved by emotion or excited by an idea. Unexpected intrusion of outsiders (plumber, etc.) need not necessarily curb this enthusiasm.

10. The less a teacher talks the better the teacher. Don't feed then; elicit from them. Learning is a process of mutual discovery for teacher and pupil. Keep an open mind to their unexpected responses. Example: comment of boy doing math that man *has* no choice.

11. Don't allow the lesson to end on the wrong note. Example: your question "What kind of man was Frost?" elicited the answer: "The kind of man who likes to write poetry." Just then the bell rang and they were dismissed.

12. Your quick praise of pupil effort and your genuine interest in what they say are first rate! It's fine for the girls to emulate you and

for the boys to try to please you. But there are certain hazards in looking *too* attractive.

There is no question in my mind but that you are a born teacher.

Samuel Bester

A commentary on supervision and mentoring: the lesson the observer experienced

Although all formal and official observation reports must contain some kind of judgment about the teacher's "performance," it's from the specific commendations and recommendations that teachers learn. Of course, it would be naïve to think that, like their own students' getting back a test, most teachers don't immediately jump to the last lines of the official report for "their mark" – their boss's rating of their performance and progress.

But, certainly as a student teacher or relatively new teacher, once you've seen "the grade you got," you will want to approach the written report as the teaching document it can be if it has been constructed they way it should be. Chairman Bester's remark in his unofficial letter to Miss Barrett that "if you wish a personal conference, please see me" would seem to indicate that at Miss Barrett's school a conference is not required before a formal observation report; however, in many school systems, a one-on-one conference precedes the issuing of a written report.

In the conference-before-anything-in-writing procedure, everything said at the conference need not wind up in the written report (and couldn't possibly), but nothing negative should be in the report that wasn't shared during the conference. Philosophically, the written report should be a distilled reflection of the supervisory conference – something the teacher can refer to more than once as a review of the learning that took place during the conference. (Sort of like good class notes students learn to take during a lesson and from which they can study in order to clinch their learning.)

In the best case scenario, the conference is where a mentoring supervisor makes it possible for a student teacher or relatively new teacher to learn about teaching and learning. Some supervisory mentors make it a point of purposely not scheduling the conference immediately after the visit (even when there is time in the schedule of both parties) because, like a good lesson, a supervisory conference benefits from being carefully planned. Conferences made up of questions planned by the supervisor are instructive, particularly when they elicit understanding on the part of the relatively new teacher.

Toward that kind of instruction, many supervisors will tell their teachers as a matter of policy that some time between the visit and the conference is needed so that observed teachers can reflect on the lesson and ready themselves to be an active part of the conference, analyzing the strengths and weaknesses of their teaching based on what they have already learned about that process. As in a good lesson carefully planned by a resourceful teacher, this kind of "homework" assignment before the conference prepares a teacher to be an active and insightful participant in the conference's dynamic.

Based on the generally positive content and tone of Chairman Bester's unofficial suggestions, it is likely that Miss Barrett opted out of a personal conference. As a supervisor and mentor, Bester appears more than satisfactory: he points out strengths and weaknesses; he explains or strongly implies why he calls them the way he does; and he encourages the continuance and the internalization of a noted strength by explaining how it produces its positive result.

This last aspect of mentoring is critical not only because a teacher's strengths need to be reinforced but also because new teachers often don't recognize some of their own strengths; in fact, sometimes they judge as a weakness in their teaching what a mentor recognizes as a strength. In the teaching process known as supervision, positives and negatives need to be pointed out and explained in a constructive and supportive way.

Although Chairman Bester's explanation for his recommendation (comment #1) that "windows should be open about 4 inches *from the top*" might not be one of the ones you predicted for this suggestion ("to avoid danger of students leaning out" – and possibly falling out from this third floor), it can probably be inferred that having the windows open at all has to do with health considerations. Fresh air keeps students awake and their mental juices flowing.

It's interesting how some new teachers can be aware that they teach in a stuffy room and yet don't seem to realize that it not only affects their comfort level and the energy of their teaching but also their students' comfort level and the extent and depth of their learning. (More experienced high school teachers who have early morning classes where students straggle in and are clearly far from completely awake sometimes wear bright shirts or blouses as "wake-up" attire for their students. Earth tones are more likely to require teacher lines like "Class to planet Earth?")

Chairman Bester does a good job supplying specific examples of strengths and weaknesses and the reasoning behind them in many of his remaining comments. You no doubt spotted them.

In his comment #2, Bester points out how too much of a good thing can subtract from rather than add to the "first-rate" strength of an external motivation. Bester also shows awareness of the games students play "to delay or avoid a lesson," running excessively with the motivation and, consequently, running away with the lesson.

In his comment #3, it would have been better if Bester had spelled out some of the reasons non-volunteers should be called on: it's their lesson, too, and they need to be viscerally reminded of that by the teacher; shy students need to be helped to overcome their shyness; students who don't trust their own thinking and leave it to the "fastest hand in the class" to carry the lesson need to know that their thinking is valued, welcomed, and required.

These reasons – and others you can think of from your reading of earlier chapters of this text – may strike you as obvious. But assumptive supervision is just as bad as assumptive teaching; since good supervision is a highly skilled act of teaching, good supervisors realize that the obvious is not necessarily obvious to the person who needs to learn the why behind the what. Bester does better when he explains in his comment #4 (made up of several points about the art of questioning): "thus engaging the whole class in thinking."

However, in this same comment #4, Bester is guilty of assumptive teaching in his mentoring, making the assumption that the answer the teacher wants is "obviously" a "yes." Actually, he cannot know that for certain; sometimes, good teachers ask "yes or no" questions to feel out a class and prompt some real thinking through a well-worded follow-up question. Although teachers are generally warned against "yes or no" questions and advised to subsume them into more specifically worded critical thinking questions, the "feeling out" yes or no question may sometimes have its place in the classroom as an ice-breaker.

Similarly, Miss Barrett's use of "How do you feel about this poem?" in its very vagueness may work for some students to ease them into sharing some specific feelings that then can be followed up on ("What in the poem made you feel that way?," "Can you find a word or a line or an image in the poem that might have caused that feeling in you?"). Bester might have been less categorical in these two remarks had they first been broached during a one-on-one conference.

Particularly instructive in his comment #5 is Bester's praise of Miss Barrett's treating "suspended boy" with respect. By emphasizing that the class had missed his contribution to it, she not only places him within the larger group but validates his place in it: "You have something to contribute to others that they missed out on." Less respectful and less astute teachers might have instead pointed out all the instruction "suspended boy" missed, validating not him but his classmates – and rubbing his nose in it.

Similarly, in his comment #12, Bester zeroes in on the respect Miss Barrett shows her students through her "genuine" interest in what her students have to say and her "quick" and apparently honest praise of their efforts (no false or formulaic effusions from this inexperienced teacher). Then, very smoothly, Chairman Bester makes a connection between these positive aspects of Miss Barrett's teacher persona and the possible persona problem of "looking *too* attractive."

Looking at Bester's comments #6 and #10 together we get a clearer picture of why #10 is the more helpful and instructive of the two: Bester, in #10, goes beyond the "telling" he does in #6 (where he advises "you might try the excellent device of pretending ignorance or surprise," while assuming that Miss Barrett can infer what makes this an "excellent device").

Instead, in #10, Bester tells and *shows* that in keeping an open mind to unexpected responses (like "man has no choice") "learning is a process of mutual discovery for teacher and pupil." By asking good questions (not feeding your students *your* answers and insights) and letting the students talk aloud about what they are thinking, the teacher elicits the insights students discover they have.

In his comment #7 ("The boy next to me was doing his math"), Bester follows the mentoring pattern of first pointing out the *undesired consequence* of poor pedagogical practice, then suggesting a different practice ("It is wise for the teacher to move about the room"), and finally allowing the intelligence of the teacher to infer the desired conclusion that all students need to be involved in the lesson.

In his comment #8, Bester, it would seem, is on less solid supervisory ground ("Immediate correction of English was effected"), seemingly declaring what he considers an obvious "good" – no reasons offered. In fact, Bester implies, through his citing of three missed opportunities, that "immediate correction" of spoken English is *always* and *ever* good. Shall we agree that this is subject to collegial discussion?

However, in his comment #9, Bester does considerably better, explaining that "Enthusiasm is contagious" and, therefore, Miss Barrett's way of not being "ashamed to show" that she can be "moved by emotion or excited by an idea" is exactly the kind of modeling she should be doing as she teaches her subject to her students.

Bester's comment #11 is similar to a "commentary" point made earlier in this chapter about the value of using the concluding thought-provoking question in a lesson's plan to assess student achievement of the lesson's aim. Most importantly, students and teachers conclude a lesson; bells simply signal the end of a period.

Chairman Samuel Bester ends his unofficial letter to Miss Barrett with high praise: "there is no question in my mind but that you are a born teacher." However, teachers are not simply born; they are made. Utilizing fictional models, this book has been about the "making" of actual teachers. Collegial mentors like Chairman Bester – in fiction and in fact, in literature and in life – are a vital part of that "making" (may you have just enough of them, and may they be more than "good enough"). But just as the authors of this book's novels created their teachers, ultimately you create the teacher you will be. You are always your own work in progress.

So you think you might like to teach? As this book's 23 fictional teachers "might" say (and I'm not responsible for their dialogue): "Other than the funds – yours and the profession's! – to cover the cost of more teacher jobs, what's keeping you?"

So, go. Go and teach if you hear the calling loud and clear. And as some of my recent undergraduate and graduate students have been heard to say, "own" your teaching career, by which they also mean, I hope!, that you take your full share of the responsibility for all your students' education.

In becoming what it is you want to become – the best possible teacher you *can* be – never lose sight of the truth that the potentially great (but never perfect) teacher is always, metaphysically, on both sides of the teacher's desk. And this caution: be wary of those jaded "mentors" (fictional and otherwise; in and out of the faculty lounge) who have existed from time immemorial and should be retired immediately.

Surely you have heard the joke that so many jaded teachers tell about the poor preparation of their students (their "line" on the line of descent): the graduate professor (or the teaching assistant) blames the undergraduate professor (or the part-time adjunct) who blames the high school teacher who blames the middle school teacher who blames the elementary school teacher who blames the day care proprietor who blames the parents who live in that infamous "house that Jack built."

Be professional; don't play any of the many "blame games" that are out there – and proliferating. Expect to work hard, because you will; you will have to: *no teacher* has ever told you it's an easy life.

But if you want to make a real, and lasting, difference for the better in a world of students, say "yes!" (not "might like") to a career in teaching. And while you're at it, have the time of *your life*.

APPENDIX A

The "Education" of Rick Dadier, contemporary urban American teacher

*W*hat follows, *in sequential order, are several of the informational sections and commentaries you have read in Chapters 1 through 8 on the teaching philosophy and practice of the fictional teacher Rick Dadier (from the novel **The Blackboard Jungle**). Since Dadier is one of the two most frequently featured teachers in **So You Think You Might Like to Teach**, re-reading these originally chapter-separated informational sections and commentaries as one continuous, uninterrupted narrative may give you as a new or aspiring teacher an even fuller sense of this role model's development into a successful teacher – in short, the "education" of Rick Dadier.*

Meet Rick Dadier of *The Blackboard Jungle*

Rick Dadier is a first-year teacher with an "ed" school degree and student teaching experience in Evan Hunter's novel *The Blackboard Jungle*. Rick values his chosen profession as a high school English teacher as "worthwhile" and "worthy" and has thrown himself, as he puts it, into molding "the clay of undeveloped minds," confident of his chances of success.

Being self-evaluative by nature (a good quality in a teacher), Rick engages in periodic "musings." His thoughts take him back a year to some of his fellow "ed" course students and forward to some of his current, more veteran, colleagues. Rick wonders why different individuals decide to become teachers. Wouldn't you? Don't you?

Rick considers some of his former "ed" classmates and current colleagues to be "meatheads," yet he wonders whether it's right for him to condemn those who "drift into the teaching profession, drift into it because it offers a certain amount of paycheck-every-month security, vacation-every-summer luxury, or a certain amount of power, or a certain easy road when the other more difficult roads are so full of ruts?"

Not surprisingly, Rick doesn't consider himself a "meathead." He believes that he "had honestly wanted to teach." He also had no illusions about his own capabilities. He muses that he "could not paint, or write, or compose, or sculpt, or philosophize deeply, or design tall buildings. He could contribute nothing to the world creatively, and this had been a disappointment to him until he'd realized he could be a big creator by teaching. For here," he concludes, "were minds to be sculpted, here were ideas to be painted, here were lives to shape."

To spend his life as something like "a bank teller or an insurance salesman" had seemed an utter waste to Rick so he "seized upon teaching, seized upon it fervently, feeling that if he could take the clay of undeveloped minds, if he could feel this clay in his hands, could shape this clay into thinking, reacting, responsible citizens, he would be creating."

Although he does not yet have children of his own (his wife is pregnant), the teacher in Rick Dadier sees the necessary connection between other people's children that his colleagues teach and *his* future children that they and others like them might teach: teach unto other parents' children as you would want your children's teachers to teach unto yours.

Consequently, the thought of certain of his "ed" school classmates' becoming teachers is upsetting to Rick, but we need to get beyond Rick's feelings about the "meatheads" in education in order to examine the implied question behind his musings: what kind of person is right for "the calling" of teaching. *You* should know *whether* you are suited for teaching. *You* should know *why* you are suited for teaching. *You* should know *how* you are suited for teaching.

"Know thyself."

How "fervent" are you about teaching? How passionate are you about your subject area? How much do you enjoy being around young people, around teenagers? Do you think a lot about getting "burned out"?

"Know thyself." How seriously do you want to be a teacher? How idealistic or realistic would you say you are about your reasons for thinking you might like to become a teacher? On a scale of from 1 to 5 (with five being the most strongly felt positive feeling), you should be concerned about any scores below four.

"Know thyself." Do you see teaching, as Rick does, as a way for you to have the ability and opportunity to take and feel "the clay of undeveloped minds" in your hands and "shape this clay into thinking, reacting, responsible citizens"?

*   *   *

The divergence between a teacher's personal life and that teacher's professional pedagogical persona

No matter what the pedagogical persona a teacher adopts, every persona causes a teacher's students to be cast in particularly delineated supporting roles. For one example, there is the teacher as the "lion-tamer" and the students as lions. ("But what happens to the best lion tamer," brand-new teacher Rick Dadier asks himself, "when he puts down his whip and his chair?")

Rick Dadier actually winds up adopting a well-known teacher persona that has been recommended to him by the school's principal, Mr. Small. And it is a teacher identity quite different from Rick's own personal identity. (Rick's own wife would not recognize him.)

As *The Blackboard Jungle* summarizes it: "The first day was the all-important day. If you started with a mailed fist, you could later open that fist to reveal a velvet palm. If you let them step all over you at the beginning, there was no gaining control later. So, whereas a little Caesar was contrary to his usual somewhat easy-going manner, he recognized it as a necessity, and he felt no guilt. As Small had advised, he was showing the boys who was boss."

Your first day in front of your students is like opening night of a piece of performance art. Curtain up! By definition, you have only *one chance* to make a "first" impression on your students, and for Rick Dadier the curtain goes up on "little Caesar," a petty dictator. Rick's metaphor of a iron-mailed fist covering a velvet palm raises the question of what Rick's students' "second impression" will be of their teacher when Rick decides he can safely show his students "the real" Mr. Dadier in the classroom.

Will Rick's students be able – and willing – to trust the "truth" of this second impression, having already been "sucker-punched" by the iron-mailed fist from the first impression Rick made? It's problematic. *When* should teachers begin to "get real"? A recommendation: how about on Day 1 as soon as the classroom's "curtain" goes up and the spotlight shines on your teacher's persona?

Such metaphors as "curtain up" and "spotlight," by the way, are a reminder that good teaching, like good acting, is a prepared "performance" in a small "theater" before a specially invited "audience." Still, it is important to consider how little or much separation there should be between a teacher's character (actual basic personality) and a teacher's "character" (role being played). Actors, by the way, consider this question as well. If, like Rick, you are not a petty dictator in real life, why do you have to "play" one in the classroom? Who says you shouldn't smile in front of your students until at least three months into the school year?

Apparently, lots of veteran teachers still give this advice to starting-out teachers. Smiling shows your students that you are as human as you find *them* to be, that you are "serious" about liking them, that the classroom is a real world place in which people are honest and genuine, and that teaching and learning are often fun endeavors. Smiling helps put the "joy" in joining together to learn. Last, but far from least, smiling is a great antidote when teachers – and students – need to lighten up and diffuse tension.

So, try entering the classroom smiling. Write the word "smiles" in the margin of a student's piece of writing when what that student wrote made you smile. Smiles are good-contagious. You can catch them from your students. They can catch them from you. No teacher has ever lost a class's respect from a smile.

*　　*　　*

Face it: Rick's colleague Lou Savoldi would beg to disagree about teacher persona

The scene is the teachers' lunchroom in the novel *The Blackboard Jungle* and veteran teacher Lou Savoldi, in front of a captive audience of other teachers (in particular, novice Rick Dadier) is stating for the nth time and for all to hear his philosophy about the "correct" teacher persona. For Veteran Lou, these oft-repeated instances (always exactly repeated, as dogma usually is) of cafeteria philosophizing are always major mentoring moments for him.

But how does Lou's fatherly professional advice sit with his potential students of the craft of teaching? Well, as a person who might go into teaching, how do you feel about what teacher Lou Savoldi says? "I'm like a man in a rainstorm," Lou begins. "When the rain is coming down, I put on my raincoat. When I get home, I take off the coat and put it in the closet and forget all about it." Lou continues, "That's what I do here. I become Mr. Savoldi the minute I step through the door to the school, and I'm Mr. Savoldi until 3:25 every day. Then I take off the Mr. Savoldi raincoat, and go home, and I become Lou again until the next morning. No worries that way."

Lou Savoldi has split himself into two people with totally separate lives: there's the public persona of "Mr. Savoldi" and the private persona of "Lou." Whenever this teacher is in the "storm" of his school life, the "raincoat" of "Mr. Savoldi" completely protects the covered-up human being of "Lou." And when this man leaves school to go home, off comes his protective teacher persona and he is once again the untouched-by-his-students "Lou" – fully forgetful of any worries connected with being a teacher.

To his credit, Rick, unlike Lou, doesn't "forget all about" his life as a teacher. In fact, that large part of his life is the subject of on-going self-evaluative conversations that Rick has with himself throughout *The Blackboard Jungle.* In one of the earliest of these "musings," Rick invokes the name of perhaps that most famous fictional teacher ever: Mr. Chips from the novel *Good-bye, Mr. Chips* by the British author James Hilton.

This particular self-evaluative conversation of Rick's begins wit the notion that "whereas tough teachers were not always loved, they were always respected. He was not particularly interested in being loved. Mr. Chips was a nice enough old man, but Rick was not ready to say good-by yet. He was interested in doing his job, and that job was teaching."

And Rick comes to the conclusion that "in a vocational school you had to be tough in order to teach. You had to be tough, or you never got the chance to teach. It was like administering a shot of penicillin to a squirming, protesting three-year-old. The three-year-old didn't know the penicillin was good for him. The doctor simply had to ignore the squirming and the protesting and jab the needle directly into the quivering buttocks."

So for Rick, it's goodbye and good riddance to Mr. Chips. However, for one thing, Rick is actually inaccurate and unfair in his implied characterization of Mr. Chips as "a nice enough old man" who was "particularly interested in being loved." In "fictional" truth, Mr. Chips, just like Rick, considered student obedience to be a necessary and essential foundation for his teaching. "Honor" (what Rick calls "respect") was "granted him" afterwards, and "love" from his students was bestowed only after his young, late-in-life bride, Kathie, had a "remarkable" *softening effect* on him. (Kathie tragically dies with their first child in childbirth within two years of their marriage.)

In fact, Mr. Chips (and it is in character that we do not know his first name) "assumed" on *his* first day of teaching a facial "scowl" in order to "cover" his inner nervousness. In addition, in his early years as a teacher Mr. Chips was a "dry and rather neutral sort of person; liked and thought well of by Brookfield in general, but not of the stuff that makes for great popularity or that stirs great affection." Only after his marriage, when Mr. Chips becomes the kind of teacher "who was kind without being soft" and "who understood them well enough, but not too much" does Mr. Chips become "beloved."

To create a straw man to knock down, Rick distorts Mr. Chips' true pedagogical persona in order to bolster his argument that "in a vocational school you had to be tough in order to teach." His disservice to a "kind without being soft" Mr. Chips does little to persuade us. Also, what are we to make of Rick's implication that students can – and should – only love a teacher in retrospect (the "one-day-way-in-the-future-you'll-thank-me" school of teaching, so, clearly, "today" is not going to be that day)?

A last point on this soul-searching of Rick's: just how apt is Rick's doctor/penicillin, teacher/learning metaphor? Any good dictionary's definition of the verb "to educate" makes it clear that teachers are *not* engaged in "the filling in of an empty vessel" (the student) with all kinds of "stuff that is good for you." Nor are they consumed with writing on students' minds as if those minds were "blank slates" to be filled in. Instead, when good teachers "educate," they are literally engaged in "a leading out."

*   *   *

The narrative of Rick Dadier's first day as a teacher

In an early scene in *The Blackboard Jungle*, Rick has his students working on that traditional opening day activity of filling out attendance cards. For those students who have come unprepared with any writing implement, Rick has thought to bring a supply of pencils from home. The scene shows in action and interaction the teacher persona that Rick has decided to adopt as a brand-new teacher.

When Rick makes an offer of pencils to anyone who is unprepared, one of the teenage students toward the back of the room (a husky boy named Sullivan) calls out, "I do, teach." Rick's immediate and angry reaction is to say, "Let's knock off this 'teach' business right now. My name is Mr. Dadier. You call me that, or you'll learn what extra homework is."

Rick's sudden fury surprises the class. As for Sullivan's response it's, "Sure, Mr. Dadier." When Rick then says to the boy, "Come get your pencil," Sullivan "rose nonchalantly." Rick notices that Sullivan is older than the other boys in this all-boy class, and "spotted him immediately as a left-backer, a troublemaker, the kind Small had warned against."

In a white tee shirt and tight dungarees, his hands shoved down into his back hip pockets, Sullivan "strode to the front of the room, taking the pencil gingerly from Rick's hand." Smiling, he says, "Thanks, teach."

"What's your name?" Rick asks, and the boy, smiling again (or still), responds, "Sullivan." (It is at this point in the narrative that we're told that Sullivan's hair "was red, and a spatter of freckles crossed the bridge of his nose. He had a pleasant smile, and pleasant green eyes.")

"How would you like to visit me after school is out today, Sullivan?" Rick asks, and the boy, still (or again) smiling answers, "I wouldn't." This teacher-student dialogue ends with Rick's saying, "Then learn how to use my name."

"Sure," Sullivan says. "He smiled again, a broad insolent smile, and then turned his back on Rick, walking lazily to his seat at the rear of the room."

By the end of this incident, Rick feels he has "lost some ground in the encounter with Sullivan," which may also mean that he has lost some ground with the class. But what does it mean to Rick to have "lost some ground"? Rick's angry reaction to Sullivan's game-playing – "his sudden fury surprising the class" – shows us how seriously Rick takes both the philosophy and practice of "in loco parentis."

It's a given to Rick that Sullivan's teachers, like Sullivan's parents, deserve genuine respect. Yet, from the very beginning to the very end of the scene in the novel this young man's verbal language ("teach"), his body language (turning his back on Rick and "walking lazily to his seat at the rear of the room"), and his facial expressions ("a broad insolent smile") paint a picture of dismissive disrespect. Since Rick wants to see himself as a tough teacher, and tough teachers are "always respected," even the slightest disrespect or false "show" of respect on the part of a student would mean to Rick that he has not succeeded in hiding his vulnerable "easy-going nature" under a believable tough exterior.

Rick responds as we would expect someone working on a tough professional teacher persona to respond: "Let's knock off this 'teach' business right now. My name is Mr. Dadier. You'll call me that or you'll learn what extra homework is." (An unfortunate, yet logical, inference that many students even today make from this tactic is that homework is, indeed, a kind of punishment, and additional "sentencing" will be meted out to fit the crime.)

Concluding the confrontation with Sullivan and laying the groundwork for a brief lecture Rick feels he needs to give in order to gain back lost ground with the entire class, Rick asks Sullivan, "How would you like to visit me after school is out today?" – to which, still smiling, the boy answers, "I wouldn't." Rick counters with, "Then learn how to use my name." Sullivan, in a "show" of respect, tellingly has the last word – the monosyllabic "Sure" as he smiles his insolent smile, turns his back on the teacher, and walks lazily back to his seat.

Rick's musings after the encounter with Sullivan – to which the entire class was witness – prompt him to decide to give the class a brief lecture. In his preparatory musings, Rick had remembered Bob Canning, an ed school grad in the class before Rick's who, like Rick, had also gone on to teach in a vocational school, but only to leave the job after five months.

Rick recalls that "Bob had allowed the boys to call him 'Bob,' a real nice friendly gesture. The boys had all just loved good old 'Bob.' The boys loved good old 'Bob' so much that they waited for him on his way to the subway one night, and rolled him and stabbed him down the length of his left arm. Good old bleeding 'Bob.'" The "pal persona." Rick vowed to himself that he would not make the same mistake.

This is Rick's brief lecture: "To begin with, as I've already told you, there'll be none of this 'teach' stuff in my classroom. I'll call you by your names, and you'll call me by mine. Common courtesy." He paused to let the point sink in. "I've also told you," he concluded, "that there will be no calling out. If you have anything to say, you raise your hand. You will not speak until I call on you. Is that clear?" The boys make no comment, and Rick takes their silence for understanding.

Apparently, Rick believes that within the confines of the student-teacher relationship, "common courtesy" (though it seems not that common in Rick's new school) would require his students to address him with the honorific "Mr." in front of his surname; at the same time, Rick finds nothing improper in addressing these adolescent boys directly by *only* their last names. On the other hand, in certain contemporary schools, teachers are encouraged by the administration to let their students call them by their given name. Know your school, and know whether you and its "culture" are a comfortable fit.

In *The Blackboard Jungle,* the clear implication from Rick's recollection of the story of Bob Canning is that allowing students to call you by your given name, as though you were their pal and, thus, not an authority figure like a parent ("in loco parentis"), is just asking for trouble – trouble like a pre-meditated physical attack and robbery. "Rick would not make the same mistake."

From the authoritative tone of Rick's lecture ("Is that clear?") and from such details as the hand-raising requirement and the no-calling-out rule, it *is* "clear" that Rick really means business. However, since "business" is a transaction that takes both a seller and a buyer, it seems problematic that Rick's students are "buying" quite yet. The sound of silence doesn't only or necessarily mean consent.

What "perspective" do you want your students to have when they look at you? (It might help you to note your reaction to Bob Canning's "mistake" and Rick's taking it as an object lesson.) How can a teacher be friendly with students in the classroom and in the school building without becoming their "pal"?

Finally, what decisions have you made or might make on such classroom protocol and procedure issues as how you and your students address each other and whether students will need to be called on before they can make a contribution to whole class instruction? (It is not too soon to reflect on how you plan to address this issue of teacher and student "address" and what your ultimate decision says about how you see your persona and its impact on the teacher-student relationship.)

*   *   *

The games Rick Dadier and his students play

If you have ever been on the Teacher end of a game we can call "Me?" (or "Who, Me?"), the following brief dialogue from Evan Hunter's novel *The Blackboard Jungle* will sound familiar. A little bit into teacher Rick Dadier's first meeting with his class at the all-boys vocational high school Manual Trades, Rick notices that the room is somewhat stuffy. Rick could say something like *"Would someone open a window in here"* and risk "a mad scramble to the windows," but Rick knows from his education courses how to do this kind of thing "according to the book": you choose one student.

Rick clearly points to a male student sitting up front near his desk and asks: "What's your name?" The boy looks frightened, "as if he had been accused of something he hadn't done" and responds, "Me?"

Rick no doubt nods his head affirmatively as he answers, "Yes, what's your name?" And the boy ends the exchange with his surname: "Dover."

A few minutes later, Rick directly asks another male student to collect the attendance-taking cards the students have been busy filling out. As this second boy is "picking up the cards dutifully," Rick interrupts him to ask *his* name, and the boy answers, "Me?"

Since there is absolutely no doubt in these two instances about who is being addressed, the question "Me?" is, in fact, the game "Me?" However, because this is Rick Dadier's first day on the job, it will take him a little while to realize the real meaning of this game *as it is played in his school*. Rick muses that the answer "irritated him a little, but that was because he did not yet know 'Me?' was a standard answer at Manual Trades High School, where a boy always presupposed his own guilt even if he were completely innocent of any misdemeanor." Is it thus in schools you are familiar with?

When teachers ask a question, it's important that they quickly assess that the question has been understood with the same meaning and in the same spirit that it was asked. Experience shows that it can take some time for this practice to become habitual for new teachers. Until then, a teacher's wanting to learn a student's name may be heard by some students as the opening to an interrogation that ends with "guilty as charged."

*   *   *

Five clichéd and disrespectful-of-students formulas for establishing discipline

Seen disrespectfully by some of its teachers as a "pit" or a "jungle," North Manual Trades is the setting for a number of clichéd "formulas" for establishing discipline among the students. Author Evan Hunter gives these discipline approaches such cutesy titles as Clobbering, Slobbering, Slumbering . . . .

Clobbering: As he periodically explains to his colleagues in the teachers' lunchroom, physical education teacher and coach Captain Schaefer is a prime believer that one should: "Clobber the bastards. It's the only thing that works. What do you think happens at home when they open their yaps? Pow, right on the noggin. That's the only language they understand." Clobbering is considered "in loco parentis" at its best by this high school teacher.

Even a non-physical teacher like Rick Dadier can understand that a teacher's urge to clobber a teenage student may often be present not too far below the teacher's professional surface – particularly in the context of such a highly physical domain as a school's body-oriented gymnasium or athletic field. However, Rick believes he could not "in all honesty, picture himself doing that" – even though "it was sometimes more difficult not to strike than it would have been to strike, and the consequences be damned."

Slobbering: Another method of discipline at North Manual Trades was Slobbering. It worked particularly well when used by a female teacher because it coupled a teacher's "I'm-touched-to-the-quick" facial expression with her verbal complaint about the ingratitude of her all-boys' class. The Slobberer whines, "After all I've done for you, you give me this treatment" – and, perhaps because of the boys' innate chivalry, a bunch of hoodlums is made to feel like heels. (The most common form of male Slobbering, one that might appeal to a group of boys' sense of fraternal spirit with their teacher, would sound like: "Come on, fellows, give me a break. I'm just a poor slob trying to do a job, that's all.")

Slumbering: The Slumberer, in sharp contrast to the Clobberer and the Slobberer, treats the whole question of discipline as a non-existent problem: He chooses to ignore the situation and proceeds to teach from the start of the period to the ending bell – and if no one pays any attention to what he is teaching, well, that's just too bad. He's there to teach, they're there to learn, and as long as he's done what he's being paid to do, he's done his job. Just as some people sleep-walk, the Slumberer sleep-teaches.

Rumbling: While the Slumberer knows there is no discipline whatsoever in his classroom and is okay with that, the Rumbler is a teacher exactly like the Slumberer except for one thing: the Rumbler invariably complains about the lack of school discipline at the end of each sleep-teaching day. He complains to his wife, to the department chair, to the principal, even. The Rumbler can even be heard complaining to himself when there is no one else around to listen. Never blaming himself, the Rumbler especially blames last year's Slumberers who allowed such a "shocking" disciplinary problem to develop.

Fumbling: The Fumbler is a teacher who simply does not know what to do about discipline. (Rick early on in *The Blackboard Jungle* considers himself a Fumbler.) Fumblers keep trying – first this way, then that way – hoping that someday they will miraculously hit upon the "cure-all" for the discipline problem. Although some Fumblers eventually work out a solution for themselves, many Fumblers become proponents of either clobbering, or slobbering, or slumbering, or rumbling.

It would seem that for some of Rick's colleagues at North Manual Trades (and for some people in the general population), there is an underlying assumption that schools in urban areas are *filled* with "problem students." A similar "given" about middle school students (urban, and suburban, and exurban) is that, first, their young age and, later, their "raging hormones" are the problem.

All starting-out teachers need to be aware of any assumptions they may have about a school's "student body" and the implications these assumptions have for their teacher persona and for their planning and teaching. Although some teachers find it extremely difficult to teach students with psychological or emotional or family problems, others do not; in fact, they thrive on it.

Whichever teacher you are, all of your students deserve understanding and the full resources of the school to address their needs. *Doing nothing more than saying* that these students "*are* problems" is to brand them and dismiss them. *And to say* that an entire group of students "*is* a problem class" *and to stop there* is to ignore the human mix of individuals that shakes and stirs a class. The solution to the so-called "problem class" is to work with, and on, the "elements" producing the wrong kind of "chemistry," not simply to bemoan the poor chemistry.

We all recognize that there are students who *have* problems but do not *cause* problems. We also know that there are students with problems who *make* problems for some, though not all, of their teachers. When they do this, they are also *making problems for other students and entire classes.* But teachers must also look at their personas, their content material, and their planning and teaching if we are to more fully understand why certain students are wreaking havoc in one classroom while working at learning in the room of the teacher next door.

As to an entire school's having "a discipline problem," that's a whole other *matter* – a matter of *the school's* leadership, its instructional philosophy, its staffing methods, its managing and monitoring of its programs – and we need to find all of this out. These are large matters, big deals.

When the author of *The Blackboard Jungle* turns the spotlight on such disciplinarians as the Clobberer, the Slobberer, the Slumberer, the Rumbler, and the Fumbler, he makes certain to have Rick Dadier call a number of them "degrading." All also have in common that they deal with discipline not as a subject to be addressed proactively but as a problem to be solved after the fact. Not one of these five discipline categories captures an approach that is "problem preventive," that actually sets out to "establish" *a disciplined class of students.* Even the Fumbler's attempts to do this are more "hit or miss" than well planned.

The field of education needs to be doing more than responding to "sickness"; it needs to be promoting "wellness," an orientation already under way in the field of medicine.

APPENDIX B

The "Education" of E. R. Braithwaite, contemporary urban British teacher

*W*_{hat} *follows, in sequential order, are many of the informational sections and commentaries you have read in Chapters 1 through 8 on the teaching philosophy and practice of the fictional teacher E. R. Braithwaite (from the novel **To Sir, With Love**). Since Braithwaite is one of the two most frequently featured teachers in **So You Think You Might Like to Teach**, re-reading these originally chapter-separated informational sections and commentaries as one continuous, uninterrupted narrative may give you as a new or aspiring teacher an even fuller sense of this role model's development into a successful teacher – in short, the "education" of E. R. Braithwaite.*

Earning the "love" in *To Sir, With Love*

In Bess Streeter Aldrich's novel *Miss Bishop*, the president of Midwestern College tells Ella Bishop why he is offering her a job teaching English grammar at the same secondary school she has just completed being a student in; one of his reasons is that she has "a keen interest" in her fellow man, something which seems to him to be "the very soul of the teaching profession."

Also not surprisingly, this is one of the key qualities that the students of the East London high school in the highly autobiographical novel *To Sir, With Love* come to recognize and honor in *their* teacher, Mr. Braithwaite. Their tribute occurs at the end of the novel when the graduates present Braithwaite with a "parcel" that has a large label pasted on it "inscribed 'TO SIR, WITH LOVE' and underneath, the signatures of all of them."

Braithwaite has come to think of his students as his "children." And when Miss Bishop retires from teaching after a long and happy "life in school," she feels "like a mother" as "she watched the last child break the tie which bound it to home."

As a starting-out teacher, E. R. Braithwaite loses at the games he plays with his students and those they play with him

In *To Sir, With Love* ("based on a true story" of Braithwaite's experiences in his first year of teaching), brand-new teacher Braithwaite gets some early advice from a veteran colleague. The "veteran" teacher tells him: "Me, I was born around hereabouts and they know it, so I can give as good as I get. Don't take any guff from them . . . or they'll give you hell. Sit heavily on them at first; then, if they play ball, you can always ease up."

The language of game-playing is so comfortably embedded in our day-to-day conversations that even this quickly and easily given piece of advice from veteran teacher to novice is replete with direct and indirect game references: "Give as good as you get." "Don't take any guff from them." "They'll give you hell." "Sit heavily on them at first." "Then, if they play ball . . . ." "You can always ease up."

Soon after being shown "the way," Braithwaite decides to assess his students' knowledge of "weights and measures" by asking them which ones they can identify. One of the male students, bypassing Braithwaite's hand-raising rule, calls out a response: "Yeah, I know. Like heavyweight, light-heavy, cruiserweight, middle, light bantam, fly-weight, feather weight." Author Braithwaite tell us that "the student held up both hands like a toddler in kindergarten and was playfully counting off on his fingers" and that when he finished, the class laughed and "at that he stood up and bowed to them with mock gravity."

Certainly the student's body language demonstrates a desire on his part to delay Braithwaite's assessment of his class's knowledge of weights and measures. With the grabbed-at spotlight on him, the student plays to an audience of his peers: he counts off on his fingers each "weight" from the unanticipated subject arena of boxing and he acknowledges the approving laughter with a stand-up bow of "mock gravity." Not "smart" about the realm of weights and measures that Braithwaite was assessing, the student plays the "smart-aleck."

But what if the student had responded only verbally – and with no obvious or apparent attitude or tone? Technically (that is to say, strictly speaking), the boxing categories the student rattles off *are* measurements of "weights."

Even if the teacher were to infer an intention on the student's part to be "too clever by half," would you as a new teacher just meeting your students for the first time choose to respond in a negative way based on that inference? Need your reaction be anything more than an acknowledgment of the technical correctness of the student's seven correct boxing weights? Or, perhaps, a possible compliment for the student's unexpected right answer is in order – along with a reminder not to call out. Better still, consider offering up the student's response to the class for the rest of the students to respond to and comment on.

So, just where is the line between "smart" and "smart-aleck" – and how carefully should teachers be looking for it? Braithwaite's actual reaction, it turns out, is to acknowledge *to himself* that the student's verbal response was "really very funny, and in another place, at another time, I, too, would have laughed as uproariously as the rest." However, Braithwaite also feels personally disrespected by what he sees as the student's playfully calculated opening move in a game – a "fighting" response in more ways than one.

"Are you interested in boxing?" Braithwaite asks the student in his opening "countermove" – and the game of "give as good as you get" is under way. "Well," Braithwaite continues, "if you have at least learned to apply the table [of weights and measures] in that limited respect, it cannot be said that you are altogether stupid . . . ."

Braithwaite's countermove is a poor one. His put-down of the student is an emotional *reaction*, not a professional *response*. Coming from the anger in his heart rather than from a considered idea in his head, Braithwaite's opening salvo is a tactic ungrounded in any carefully devised overall game plan or strategy; its origins are in Braithwaite's desire to "give as good as you get" by belittling the student. However, in all psychological game-playing between human beings, moves floating free of a foundational strategy can get picked off one by one by an opponent who knows what he's up to (his own strategy) and where he's going with it.

It is not surprising, then, that most of the other students in the class (appreciative spectators to the game) support the Student side with laughter: they see their fellow student as winning. Being a novice at the game that he has started to play (the game of "give as good as you get"), Braithwaite resorts to sarcasm, which, unlike verbal irony, is by definition "mean-spirited." Publicly shaming a student he barely knows in front of the student's peers, Braithwaite couples the backhanded compliment "you have at least learned to apply the table in that limited respect" with the zinger "it cannot be said that you are altogether stupid." By simply reacting without any overall strategy, Braithwaite is already losing this game badly – and he knows it.

So what should Braithwaite do now in order to save himself both professionally and personally? The author Braithwaite tells us that he knew that he "had to do something, anything, and quickly. They were challenging my authority, probably with no feeling of antipathy to myself, but merely to maintain a kind of established convention of resistance to a new teacher, watching closely for any sign of weakness or indecision . . . ."

Thinking that "a fight was what they wanted," Braithwaite decides to continue game-"boxing" with the class and give his new students the fight they want: "That's enough!" he shouts, his voice sharp and loud enough to cut off the class's laughter.

Braithwaite recognizes that the game "give as good as you get" is more specifically the game we can call, as he does, "Resistance to a New Teacher." No one has a copyright on this game, as you might well know from your own experiences in the classroom as a student or teacher.

The game "Resistance to a New Teacher" is a classic. Played by students around the world, it is not – it is critical to note – meant to be taken *personally* by a new teacher. These students don't know *you* long enough and well enough to be out to get *you*! (Of course, over time, students' games can be decidedly personal if a teacher's behavior is seen as "*you're* asking for it.") However, in the case of Braithwaite's classroom, the conventional game of "resistance to a new teacher" is being traditionally re-enacted to challenge and test his professional confidence in his own authority. For many teachers just starting out, this is a "rite of passage."

Responding to Braithwaite's authoritatively "sharp and loud" command of "that's enough!" the class does stop laughing; however, some students make the opposing move against Braithwaite of "not smiling now, but glaring angrily at me." Braithwaite even hears a few murmurs of cursing. Then the lunch bell rings, ending morning classes.

Lunchtime over, Braithwaite finds that his lessons pass "without incident, but unsatisfactorily." Lunchtime may be over, but the game isn't. Watching the class do its thing (its "strategy" unfolding to reveal itself to anyone really trying to figure out what was going on), Braithwaite immediately notices that "the children neither chatted nor laughed, nor in any way challenged my authority, but at the same time they were unco-operative."

Behavior problems? The students' behavior was no problem in the all-too-narrow but traditional conception of the term: "They listened to me, or did the tasks assigned to them, like automata. My attempts at pleasantries were received with a chilly lack of response, which indicated that my earlier remarks had got under their skin. Their silent watchfulness was getting under mine."

Although Braithwaite's "personal" moves in the game are now intentionally "pleasant," when his students react at all it is less like humans and more like robots: none of them "put themselves" into any of the "tasks" Braithwaite asks them to do. Because Braithwaite's students have taken his game-playing *personally*, Teacher and Student sides are at a standoff, with each under the other's skin. However, because these students are much more experienced at game-playing than he is and are foiling Braithwaite's objective, Teacher is losing the game.

Perhaps you have heard the term "classroom management" a couple of times (or more!) since you started to think about being a teacher. What Braithwaite *has achieved* in the game he got lured into is to "manage his classroom." This accomplishment, however, was at the expense of Braithwaite's truly teaching his students. Fundamentally "unco-operative," Braithwaite's students successfully forestall the kind of true teaching and learning that Braithwaite hopes to accomplish.

Prospective and relatively new teachers often confuse classroom management with teaching. *They are not the same.* Being a teacher is about teaching other human beings – call them "the class." A "classroom," unlike those who inhabit it, is a place – not the people in it. Empty classrooms can be locked with a key; empty classes can be "unlocked" – that is, opened for teaching. Successful teachers rarely have "classroom management" issues because their managing of the classroom is an indirect *but natural* by-product of their successful teaching of the class. Poor teachers may learn, right away or eventually, how to manage a classroom. But they remain poor teachers.

*   *   *

Braithwaite is sent to fill a sudden teacher vacancy and his life is changed when he meets Headmaster Alex Florian of the Greenslade Secondary School

Like Rick Dadier, teacher E. R. Braithwaite feels he's not financially in a position to turn down any job offer. (Both in the real world and the real world of novels, it's not often that we are.) But unlike Rick, Braithwaite *is given* that option by Alex Florian, headmaster of a British secondary school. Braithwaite, in fact, goes on to consider saying "no, thank you" to an "official appointment" for a position the previous occupant abruptly resigned from.

Braithwaite's day began with Mr. Florian's meeting briefly with him and telling him, as Braithwaite relates it to another teacher a little while later, to "take a look around to sort of see what's going on" before he decides whether to accept the appointment.

Braithwaite goes off on his own and on the basis of what he experiences that morning of the school's building and its students and teachers, he rather unenthusiastically decides to "have a shot" at the job: "I wanted this job badly and I was quite prepared to do it to the best of my ability, but it would be a job, not a labor of love." When you make this kind of distinction, you are far from having found your best-of-all-possible schools.

But when Braithwaite returns to the headmaster's office, where he had had *no interview* and, therefore, no opportunity to ask fact – earlier only told Braithwaite that "things are done here somewhat differently from the usual run," proceeds to provide answers to such unasked questions as: "what is this school all about, anyway?" and "what are the students like?" and "how do you and your staff go about doing what you do here?" and "what is it you hope to accomplish?"

In fact, Mr. Florian's "interview with himself" is more of a mission statement on his school's "conceptual framework" than it is the kind of interview Chair Stanley had with Rick Dadier in *The Blackboard Jungle*.

"You may have heard," Mr. Florian tells Braithwaite, "some talk about this school, Braithwaite. We're always being talked about, but unfortunately, most of the talk is by ill-informed people who are intolerant of the things we are trying to do here." To set the record straight for Braithwaite, Mr. Florian states up front that "the majority of the children here could be generally classified as difficult, probably because in Junior school they have shown some disregard for, or opposition to, authority."

Mr. Florian goes on to say, however, that "whether or not that authority was well-constituted is beside the point; it is enough to say that it depended largely on fear, either of the stick or some other form of punishment. In the case of these children it failed. We in this school believe that children are merely men and women in process of development; and that that development, in all its aspects, should be neither forced nor restricted at the arbitrary whim of any individual who by some accident of fortune is in a position to exercise some authority over them."

Mr. Florian then dramatically specifies why punishment (or the threat of it) of these children for their "lack of interest" in school work is "unlikely" to bring out the best of them: "A child who has slept all night in a stuffy, overcrowded room, and then breakfasts on a cup of weak tea and a piece of bread, can hardly be expected to show a sharp, sustained interest in the abstractions of arithmetic, and the unrelated niceties of correct spelling."

As to the school behavior of such children, Mr. Flolrian sees it as "part of the general malaise which affects the whole neighborhood" that they live in and "produces a feeling of insecurity among the children." Instead of using coercion to discourage anti-social conduct, Greenslade Secondary School tries to give its students "affection, confidence, and guidance, more or less in that order, because experience has shown us that those are their most immediate needs."

Finally, Mr. Florian counters the talk of the ill-informed about Greenslade when he states that "it is said that here we practice free discipline. That's wrong, quite wrong. It would be more correct to say that we are seeking, as best we can, to establish disciplined freedom, that state in which the child feels free to work, play and express himself without fear of those whose job it is to direct and stimulate his efforts into constructive channels."

What will be Braithwaite's role be if he accepts the appointment to Greenslade? Mr. Florian makes it clear that "as teachers, we can help greatly if we become sufficiently important" to these children; "important enough for our influence to balance or even outweigh the evil . . . . Remember, they're wonderful children when you get to know them, and somehow, I think you will. Good luck."

Whether your professional goal is to find "a job" or "*the* job," the process of job-hunting must include learning as much as you can about a particular school, department, student body, faculty, or educational leader. This last is really important; the principal of a school sets the tone of and for the school. In effect, you need to know exactly *why* you would accept or decline a position should one be offered to you.

A long look at E. R. Braithwaite's desire to become the best possible teacher he can be

E. R. Braithwaite's desire to become the best possible teacher he can be is, in fact, the story line of *To Sir, With Love*. Fairly late in the narrative, Braithwaite demonstrates that he understands that a teacher must always be a continual learner when he explains to a colleague why he has not even thought about moving on to some so-called "better school."

His reason, he says, is that he's "only just begun teaching, you know, not more than a few months. It hardly seems enough to decide whether or not I'm really much good at it." And, he continues, "I may be able to get to terms with these kids, but it might be quite different with others. I think I ought to stay where I am and learn a little more about the job and my own abilities before I think of moving."

Early in the narrative, having completed his studies to become a teacher, Braithwaite is on his way to an officially promised "appointment" to a school where a teacher has suddenly quit – no advance notice, no warning. Knowing little about the school but badly needing the job, Braithwaite is prepared to accept the assigned position. However, when he goes to meet with the school's headmaster, Alex Florian, as a matter of form the headmaster unexpectedly says: "We're glad to have you. I hope that when you've had a chance to look at us you'll be just as pleased to stay."

Braithwaite, appreciating the direct welcome of the first sentence but surprised by the implied option of the second, hastens to reassure the headmaster: "Not much doubt about that, Sir." That sounds like the practical or politically correct response, but consider how would you react and respond if the principal of the school you had been "assigned" to as your first school proposed something like the following: "I think it would be best if you had a good look around the school first, and then we'll talk about it," says the headmaster and your future principal.

He then continues: "things are done here somewhat differently from the usual run, and many teachers have found it, shall we say, disquieting. Wander around just as you please, and see what's going on, and if you then decide to remain with us, we'll talk about it after lunch."

Wouldn't it be something if all new teachers had this option and opportunity? They might not wind up working in a school or department or for someone that they were philosophically or otherwise incompatible with.

As it turns out, Braithwaite, in fact, does find somewhat "disquieting" what he glimpses and overhears as he "wanders around." Nevertheless, because he desperately needs the job (having been repeatedly and blatantly discriminated against in England because of his skin color when he sought work as a communications engineer, his original vocation), Braithwaite accepts the appointment to a new career and begins teaching his class that very day.

Braithwaite's feeling "disquieted" is the result of a palpable *disconnect* between his attitude, experiences, and success as a student and what he sees and overhears as he has "a good look around." As he checks out a school building that he himself finds "depressing, like a prison," Braithwaite cannot help but compare his own experiences as a student with what he observes among the student body of what will be his first school as a teacher. In similar circumstances, you, too, would quite naturally compare and contrast, evaluate and judge the schools you've experienced as a student with those you are considering as a prospective teacher.

Early on in the narrative of *To Sir, With Love*, Braithwaite shares memories of his own student days. A black man born and reared in British Guiana, Braithwaite also compares these memories with what he sees and hears during his "good look around" his future school as a teacher – and the comparison leaves him depressed. He tells us: "My depression deepened and I thought how very different all this was from my own childhood schooldays spent in warm sunny Georgetown. There, in a large rambling wooden schoolhouse, light and cool within, surrounded by wide, tree-shaded lawns on which I had romped with my fellows in vigorous contentment, I spent rich, happy days, filled with the excitement of learning, each new little achievement a personal adventure and a source of satisfaction to my interested parents."

Braithwaite concludes this memory with two questions he has already implied an answer to: "How did these East London children feel about coming to this forbidding-looking place, day after day? Were they as eagerly excited about school as I had been when a boy?"

Braithwaite's two questions about his future students and their feelings about school are posed rhetorically; yet the fact that he asks them in the context of his own very positive school memories and calls the East London school building a "forbidding-looking place" strongly suggests the answers would be in the negative. Still, most of the teachers depicted in *To Sir, With Love*, we learn as the narrative continues, do right by their students – that unsuccessful teacher that Braithwaite replaces, notwithstanding.

But what does "doing right" by students consist of? How much of an intuitive understanding does Braithwaite demonstrate in his words and actions on Day 1 as he addresses his students for the first time? Standing in front of his desk, Braithwaite waits until the students have settled in their seats and tries "to inject as much pleasant informality as possible" into his voice: "The Headmaster," he begins "has told you my name, but it will be some little while before I know all yours, so in the meantime I hope you won't mind if I point at you or anything like that; it will not be meant rudely."

Braithwaite next shares his plan for the day: "I do not know anything about you or your abilities, so I will begin from scratch. One by one I'll listen to you reading; when I call your name will you please read anything you like from any one of your schoolbooks."

Braithwaite then adds in the same vein, "Our arithmetic lesson will be on weights and measures. As with our reading lesson, I am again trying to find out how much you know about it and you can help by answering my questions as fully as you are able."

Although it would be natural for you to be curious about whether Braithwaite's first interactions with his class worked (for teaching and learning), you do not in reality need to know the "outcomes" of his efforts in order to evaluate their "potential." To begin with, Braithwaite has physically and symbolically removed a barrier and narrowed the distance between himself and the students by positioning himself in front of the teacher's desk. (Would it be better – the barrier of the teacher's desk still behind him – for Braithwaite to sit in a chair or desk-chair at student level? Some American teachers would say so.)

Braithwaite tells us that he purposely chose an informal tone of voice for his "first impression" on his students rather than a formal "address" with its connotation of "talking down from on high." Similarly, because he expects to receive respect from the members of his class Braithwaite *shows* them respect as human beings and as young adults.

Repeatedly, Braithwaite treats these adolescents like the true students he hopes they will become: he provides an educational explanation for the teaching procedure he plans to follow, one that will address their needs ("so I will begin from scratch"); he anticipates a possible negative misinterpretation of his pointing to students until he learns their names ("it will not be meant rudely"); he admits that he, too, is human ("it will take some while before I . . ."); he models good manners ("please," "I hope you won't mind"); and he communicates that he believes in giving students free choice within educationally sound limits ("read anything you like from any one of your schoolbooks").

Understanding the importance of assessment for the purposes of reviewing, reinforcing, and re-teaching, Braithwaite proceeds to apply to an arithmetic assessment the same teaching procedure he used for an earlier reading assessment; this shows, in addition, that he recognizes an opportunity to make a meaningful connection between two "different" parts of the lesson ("I am again trying to find out how much you know").

Nevertheless, the key strength of Braithwaite's respectful opening conversation with his new students is that it *is* a conversation, not a formal lecture. His purpose is to let them know at the very start of their teacher-student relationship that not only does he want to help them but also that he understands that he needs *their* help (not just their co-operation) in order to be of any real *service* to them as people with lives and futures ("and you can help by . . .").

Clearly, on his first day as their teacher, Braithwaite strives to convey to his students that he is human and that his heart is in the right place. With the passing of time, Braithwaite's teaching style and his relationship with his students passes through three distinct phases. "I tried very hard to be a successful teacher with my class," he tells us, "but somehow, as day followed day in painful procession, I realized that I was not making the grade."

As you move with Braithwaite through these three phases, what would you say Braithwaite is learning about being a "successful" teacher? Is this new knowledge applicable elsewhere – to other students in other schools (and to other teachers like yourself)? What else, would you say, does Braithwaite need to learn?

In Phase 1, Braithwaite's students would give him "the silent treatment," and "during that time, for my first few weeks, they would do any task I set them without question or protest, but equally without interest or enthusiasm; and if their interest was not required on the task in front of them they would sit and stare at me with the same careful, patient attention a birdwatcher devotes to the rare feathered visitor . . . . It made me nervous and irritable, but I kept a grip on myself" and "took great pains with the planning of my lessons, using illustrations from the familiar things of their own background . . . . I created varying problems within the domestic framework, and tried to encourage their participation, but it was as though there was a conspiracy of disinterest, and my attempts at informality fell pitifully flat."

In the second "and more annoying phase of their campaign," Braithwaite's students would give him "the noisy treatment"; for example, when Braithwaite would speak or read aloud "someone would lift the lid of a desk and let it fall with a loud bang; the culprit would merely sit and look at me with wide innocent eyes as if it were an accident. They knew as well as I did that there was nothing I could do about it, and I bore it with as much a show of aplomb as I could manage. One or two such interruptions during a lesson was usually enough to destroy its planned continuity, and I was often driven to the expedient of . . . substituting some form of written work; they could not write and bang their desks at the same time."

Also during the noisy treatment phase, Braithwaite could not talk as much with the class "about everything and anything"; the bell would less frequently find teacher and students "deep in interested discussion," with Braithwaite "showing them that the whole purpose of their education was the development of their own thinking and reasoning."

By Phase 3, "there was growing up between the children and myself a real affection which I found very pleasant and encouraging. Each day I tried to present to them new facts in a way which would excite and stimulate their interest, and gradually they were developing a readiness to comment and also a willingness to tolerate the expressed opinions of others; even when those opinions were diametrically opposed to theirs . . . . I was learning from them as well as teaching them. I learned to see them in relation to their surroundings, and in that way to understand them."

APPENDIX C

The 19 Novels at the Heart of This Book

Once you have completed or read as much of this book as you want or need to, you might consider really getting to know the 23 fictional teachers found in its pages by reading some of the works of literature they appear in. There is nothing like a novel that features a teacher for having an extended educational conversation with – and there are scores of teacher and school novels out there just waiting to be read, enjoyed, savored, and learned from. As you continue your teacher education on the job, don't forget these fictional teachers as future colleagues and mentors. A reading list of the 19 novels at the heart of this book follows in the order first mentioned:

The Blackboard Jungle by Evan Hunter, United States, 1954

The Friend of Women by Louis Auchincloss, United States, 2007

Theophilus North by Thornton Wilder, United States, 1973

Good-bye, Mr. Chips by James Hilton, Great Britain, 1934

Miss Bishop by Bess Streeter Aldrich, United States. 1933

To Sir, With Love by E. R. Braithwaite, Great Britain, 1959

The Dead School by Patrick McCabe, Ireland, 1995

The Prime of Miss Jean Brodie by Muriel Spark, Great Britain, 1961

A New Life by Bernard Malamud, United States, 1961

Hard Times by Charles Dickens, Great Britain, 1854

The Longest Journey by E. M. Forster, Great Britain, 1922

The Class by Hermann Ungar, Germany, 1927
      (English translation by Mike Mitchell, 2003)

Freshman Focus by Carla R. Sarratt, United States, 2007

Schooled in Murder by Mark Richard Zubro, United States, 2008

The Misadventures of Justin Hearnfeld by Dan Elish, United States, 2008

The Rainbow by D. H. Lawrence, Great Britain, 1915

A Tree Grows in Brooklyn by Betty Smith, United States, 1943

If You Knew Me by Anne Roiphe, United States, 1993

Up the Down Staircase by Bel Kaufman, United States, 1964

9 781479 798148